WHEN
THE HEART
IS HUNGRY

Other Books by Charles L. Allen

ROADS TO RADIANT LIVING
IN QUEST OF GOD'S POWER
GOD'S PSYCHIATRY

WHEN
THE HEART
IS HUNGRY

CHRIST'S PARABLES FOR TODAY

Charles L. Allen ~ 1913 ~

FLEMING H. REVELL COMPANY

Dedicated to my brothers

Stanley F. Allen
Goodman, Mississippi

&

John R. Allen
LaGrange, Georgia

Exemplars of Romans 12:10

CONTENTS

Earthly Stories with Heavenly Meanings   11

1. THE PRICE OF THE SUPREME
   *The Parables of the Buried Treasure and
   The Pearl of Great Price*   15

2. THE FOUR WHO ARE LOST
   *The Parables of the Sheep, The Coin,
   The Two Sons*   21

3. HOW TO LOSE AND FIND GOD
   The Parable of the Prodigal Son   30

4. THE MOST HOPELESS SINNER
   The Parable of the Elder Brother   37

5. PRAY BECAUSE OF YOUR NEED
   *The Parable of the Pharisee and The
   Publican*   44

6. PRAY UNTIL YOU GET THE ANSWER
   The Parable of the Friend at Midnight   51

7. YOUR PRAYER WILL BE ANSWERED
   The Parable of the Friend at Midnight   57

8. WHEN THE HEART IS HUNGRY
   The Parable of the Great Supper   64

9. WHEN YOU ARE WOUNDED
   The Parable of the Good Samaritan   70

10. THE FOUR PEOPLE WHO GO TO CHURCH
    The Parable of the Four Soils   76

11. MAINTAIN YOUR FORGIVENESS
    The Parable of the Unmerciful Servant   83

12. BE READY FOR YOUR OPPORTUNITY
    The Parable of the Ten Bridesmaids   90

13. FINDING THE JOY OF THE LORD
    The Parable of the Talents   97

14. THE MAN GOD CALLED A FOOL
    The Parable of the Rich Farmer   104

15. REMEMBER WHO YOU ARE
    The Parable of the Unjust Steward   111

16. FOUNDATION FOR A LIFE
    The Parable of Two Builders   117

17. OUR HERE DETERMINES OUR HEREAFTER
    The Parable of the Rich Man and Lazarus   123

18. WHAT JESUS SAID ABOUT THE JUDGMENT DAY
    The Parable of the Last Judgment   129

19. His Kingdom Is Growing
   The Parable of a Grain of Mustard Seed   136

20. For Those Who Are Waiting for a Chance
   The Parable of the Laborers   142

21. Overcome the Evil of Life
   The Parable of the Wheat and the Tares   148

22. The Idea of Positive Thinking
   *The Parable of the House That Was
   Swept Clean and Left Empty*   154

EARTHLY STORIES WITH HEAVENLY MEANINGS

"EARTHLY STORIES WITH HEAVENLY MEANINGS"—THAT IS the best definition of the parables of Christ I have found. As one studies the parables, certainly he is impressed with the fact that they are "down-to-earth." They deal with the common experiences of men and minister to man's daily needs. Also, as one studies the parables he begins to see the will of God for his earthly life and the way into life that is eternal.

These studies in some of the parables are not scholarly expositions. They were first prepared as the basis of a series of Sunday *night* sermons at Grace Methodist Church in Atlanta. Perhaps a brief description of that service will help the reader to understand the messages here printed.

An average of a thousand or more people attend these services. They come not out of loyalty or a sense of duty, but rather because of a felt spiritual need. The service begins with an informal song service using the simple gospel hymns. The sermon is an effort to help and encourage and to feed the hunger of hearts of those who have come seeking and expecting help.

At the close of the sermon every Sunday night an invitation is given to kneel and pray at the altar. Over a period of nearly seven years now this opportunity for altar prayers has been given at every Sunday night service. Out of the thousand present, usually about six hundred come forward to kneel and pray as there is room at the altar. As a result of this service, many lives are changed and hungry hearts are fed.

Of course, the parables of Christ are inexhaustible in meaning. No attempt is here made to give the entire meaning of any one of those matchless stories. Rather is the aim to liven up a little of the truth of Christ found in each of the parables used, and to present the message in as simple a manner as possible.

Parts of these messages have been used in my column which appears daily on the editorial pages of *The Atlanta Constitution,* and I would like to express appreciation for permission to use the material again here.

Especially would I like to express my very deep admiration of the men of Fleming H. Revell Company, Mr. William Barbour, Sr., Mr. Wilbur Davies, Dr. Frank Mead and the many others. This is my fourth book with this firm, and our relationship has grown to be one of friendship which is one of the happier experiences of my life.

CHARLES L. ALLEN

Grace Methodist Church
Atlanta, Georgia

WHEN
THE HEART
IS HUNGRY

1. THE PRICE OF THE SUPREME

*The Parables of the Buried Treasure
and The Pearl of Great Price*
MATTHEW 13:44-46

WITH JUST A FEW WORDS JESUS COULD PAINT A COMPLETE picture. For example: "The kingdom of heaven is like unto treasure hid in a field; the which when a man hath found, he hideth, and for joy thereof goeth and selleth all that he hath, and buyeth that field."

We can easily see the picture. A tenant farmer is laboriously plowing. He finds no joy or pride in his work. The land is rocky and worn out, and it will produce very little. He is thinking of his wife and children at home. Home is a sorry little shack. His wife has not had a new dress in several years, and the last one she did get was the cheapest in the store.

For lack of proper clothes and food, his children are sickly. He doesn't have the money to buy them any toys, or even books. He cannot look forward to better times, and maybe at the end of the year his landlord will make him move. He doesn't know where else he might go. He barely ekes out an existence. Life for him is a bitter disappointment.

Suddenly his plow strikes something. Likely he curses the rocks, but he looks and sees it was not a rock. The rusty lid of an old metal box is torn out of the ground. The glint of gold catches his eye. Feverishly he pulls the dirt away from a box of buried treasure. According to the law of that day, "finders were keepers." He carefully hides the treasure, rushes to sell all he has, makes a down payment on the field.

His dreams have come true. He now has security. He can buy for his family the things they need. He can make a position of respect for himself in the community. He becomes a very happy man.

Along the same line, Jesus gives us another story. "The kingdom of heaven is like unto a merchant man, seeking goodly pearls: who, when he had found one pearl of great price, went and sold all that he had, and bought it." This man finds joy in collecting beautiful pearls and he has many of them. But in each one he sees tiny flaws, and he keeps looking and hoping to find one with which he will be entirely satisfied.

One day in the market place he sees the perfect pearl. The price is high, but without hesitation he sells all he has and buys it. There is deep soul-satisfaction in possessing something so fine and beautiful.

And Jesus gave us these two pictures to show us what it is like to possess God. Sometimes we think of religion as taking all the joy out of life but, instead, it is like finding buried treasure, like finding a perfect jewel. We remember such stories as Stevenson's *Treasure Island*, Poe's *The Gold Bug* and Alexandre Dumas', *The Count of Monte Cristo*. Even the search is exciting. Finding and possessing will send us out, as it did Archimedes, shouting, "Eureka! Eureka! I have found it."

UNSATISFIED HUNGERS

Jesus likens finding God to two men. One was plowing in the field and accidentally discovered buried treasure. The other was searching for a perfect pearl and found it. Weatherhead suggests the first man is like one outside the church, the second like one inside the church.

There is a vast multitude of people with unsatisfied hungers. Life is a hard, disappointing experience. They may live in gutters or in castles, it matters not how little or how much we have, if we fail to possess that which satisfies our deepest hungers. Many have become bitter and hopeless and find life not to be worth living. Some have been conquered by despair and have no heart and no reason to keep on trying.

In their search for satisfaction, some went off on the wrong trails. Now they see their wrongs, but upon their memories is stamped forever the shame of a miserable past. They would now like to do better but with the dirt on their souls, what is the use of trying? In youth there were dreams and stars to move toward, but the light of the stars has faded and the dreams serve only to mock and torment.

But though God is forgotten, He doesn't forget. God keeps putting unrest and dissatisfaction into that person's heart and one moment, suddenly he sees God. A God who can forgive sins, who can take the pieces of a broken life and put them back together again, who can give reason and purpose to living. The God who sent

His Son not to condemn but to save. It is like finding buried treasure. Joyously we possess it, no matter what the cost, and a new life becomes ours. We become so happy.

On the contrary, the merchant man all along had sought the "goodly pearls" and he had found many which had brought him some joy. He is like many people who are inside the church. He enjoys attending the services. He is helped by the sermons. He likes to sing and pray with others in the congregation, he gets satisfaction out of service to others. But for him there is still something lacking.

He is faithful to his work and makes a contribution to society by being a good citizen. He provides well for his family and finds joy in his home. He has friends who are loyal. But somehow, still he has not found what he wants most.

In this connection, Dr. Buttrick reminds us of Tennyson's story of The Holy Grail. One knight, riding on the quest, came upon laden fruit trees but even as he ate the fruit it turned to dust. No feeding of the body could satisfy the soul. Riding on, he found a gracious woman and a home. Surely the love of a woman and the sweet shelter of a home was what he wanted. He said: "But when I touched her, lo! she too, fell into dust and nothing, and the house became no better than a broken shed."

Only the Holy Grail could satisfy. "Goodly pearls." Paul had many good pearls but only after that day on the Damascus Road when he saw Christ and completely surrendered to Him, was life full and satisfying.

THE TREASURE IS WORTH IT

The climax in Jesus' stories of the man finding the buried treasure and in the merchant finding the pearl of great price is the eagerness with which each possessed their discoveries. Each, when he made the discovery "went and sold all that he hath." Each did it joyfully. Neither felt he was making any sacrifice because the treasure he was possessing was worth so much more than what he had to offer for it that he did not hesitate.

Jesus said the kingdom of heaven is like that. Once we see what it is worth to have God in our hearts, to have His spirit empower our lives, to follow His will, we realize that no matter what the cost, we want God above and beyond all things else. We sometimes think of religion in terms of sacrifice, duty and self-denials and we decide the price is too high. But when we really glimpse the glory of God, the price we pay becomes nothing.

The disciples "left all to follow Him." Paul surrendered all the things he had thought so highly of, saying, "But what things were gain to me, those I counted loss for Christ" (Phil. 3:7). Again and again Augustine prayed, "Make me pure . . . but not now." Certain sins he was not ready to part with. Later after he did possess Christ, he cries, "What I feared to be parted from was now a joy to surrender."

In each instance both men immediately possessed their treasures. They did not wait until a later time. There awaits each of us the "exceeding riches of His grace" . . . "The unsearchable riches of Christ." Our spiritual poverty can be taken away at once. But if we wait until we resolve every intellectual doubt, we will never have it. When we possess Christ, our doubts are then gone. We need not wait for moral reform. That, too, will come when He comes.

A man was in to see me recently saying, "More than anything else, I want the peace of God in my heart." I replied, "When really you want Him more than anything, you shall immediately have Him." When we kneel to pray, often there is some one thing which stands in our way. Do we want God enough to do what we should about that "one thing"? That is the price.

Finally, look at two fascinating young men we see walking along the pages of the New Testament. One was stoned to death by a mob. He was young and full of life, but even as he died he was able to "look steadfastly into heaven, and saw the glory of God." He prayed for those who stoned him. Even the stones of a mob could not take the peace out of his heart (Acts 7:55,59).

The other was a rich, young ruler. He wanted the life that Christ could offer, but he did not want it badly enough. There was some "one thing" he would not surrender. So he turns and goes away. He keeps what he has, but the Bible says, "he went away sorrowful" (Matt. 19:22). Truly the kingdom of God is like unto treasure—the supreme treasure of treasures. When we see that, joy and peace shall be ours—but not until then.

2. THE FOUR WHO ARE LOST

The Parables of the Sheep, the Coin,
the Two Sons

LUKE 15

ONE OF THE MOST BELOVED CHAPTERS OF THE BIBLE IS
Luke 15. I like the way it begins: "Then drew near unto
Him, all the publicans and sinners, for to hear Him."
That tells us a lot about Christ. It means that those who
had failed, realized that in Him they would find help
instead of condemnation. We are told that He was "a
friend of sinners," that He liked to eat with them, that
He gave most of His time to them. He had harsh words
for self-righteous people, but always He spoke kindly
to those who had missed the way. In fact, the word "sinner" was seldom on His lips. He thought of them as
"lost." So when the people "murmured" because He
received sinners, He told them four stories. In those
stories we see who the lost are, how they became lost,
and God's attitude toward them.

LOST THROUGH OTHER INTERESTS
First, there was the sheep that was lost. It was not a
bad sheep. No doubt it loved the shepherd just as much

as the others. The story does not imply that the sheep willfully ran away. It was out eating grass one day; it was good grass and good for him to eat it. But as he ate he so enjoyed it that he forgot the shepherd and just kept drifting away. Finally he looked up and it was dark, and the shepherd was out of sight.

That is the way a lot of people get lost. We get interested in things—even good things—and we become so absorbed that we forget to pray, we are too busy to go to church, we gradually leave God out of our lives. Then one day something happens. Maybe it is some deep sorrow or crisis, or some great need in our lives, and we realize we are not sufficient unto ourselves. But we do not know where God is or how to find Him. We are lost.

The lost sheep was still a good sheep. Just being lost did not make it mean and depraved. The shepherd leads the sheep and, being away from the shepherd, it had no guide. It did not know which way to turn. There are many people who find themselves in that situation. They do not need to be fussed at, they need to be helped.

LOST THROUGH IDLENESS

Second, a coin was lost. That does not mean that once it was silver and turned to copper. Though it was lost, it was still the same coin and just as good as it ever was. Being lost does not necessarily mean a person has thrown away all of his character, principles and ideals. A lost person may not be an immoral person. One can be lost to God and yet at the same time live an honest, decent life and treat his fellowman fairly.

The coin was lost because it was out of circulation. A coin represents service. But unless it is spent it accomplishes nothing. Now there are a lot of fine and good people who are not doing anything as far as service to God is concerned. They are like the man who buried his talents in the ground or the fig tree that produced no fruit. The highest purpose of man is to serve God. If one is not using his talents for God, then he is lost. As far as the work of God is concerned, many people are out of circulation.

Jesus knew that the attitude of the self-righteous Pharisees would only drive those further away. That such could be found only by showing them a better way to spend their lives. He knew that if once they could really see Him, what He stood for, His plans and purposes for the world, they would give themselves to Him and it would mean so much.

LOST THROUGH DESIRES

Third was the prodigal son. No doubt he was a fine young man, full of life and spirit, and wanting to live life to its fullest. Home was dull, the restraints of his father irked him, and he decided he could manage his own life.

So he goes out on his own and the only master he listens to is his own desires. He never thinks of what he ought to do; he only does what he wants to do. He never prays, "Thy will be done," instead he says, "It is my life and nobody can dictate to me." He declares his declaration of independence. He recognizes no laws but the ones he makes for himself.

He has a good time for awhile, but eventually he learns that he is not sufficient unto himself. "He begins to be in want," and he cannot supply his wants. He becomes a beggar and a beggar is never free. We read how he was "sent" by the one who answered his pleas. He was lost in the sense that he had become a slave. He gave way to his desires until eventually his desires became his master.

LOST THROUGH PRIDE

Finally, there was the "Elder Brother." He was not a bad fellow. As we read the story we find that he was in the field hard at work. In fact, we find that he worked right up to supper time. He was not a dead-beat or an immoral person. No doubt he was honest and conscientious and was a good citizen of the community. I imagine he went to church every Sunday.

Yet the elder brother was the most completely lost of the four. He was lost because he was so proud of himself. Others fell into sinful ways, but he boasted of the straight life he lived. He felt he was as good as he was supposed to be. He had no need to improve; his heart never hungered and thirsted for God; he never felt the need of kneeling at the altar. Study the lives of the true saints and you will find they felt constantly their need of God and were ever seeking to be more like Him. But the Elder Brother became satisfied with himself, and when he reached that point his progress stopped. He became lost.

So—there are the four who are lost: the one who has lost his guide, the one out of circulation, the one who has become the slave of himself, and the one who is satisfied with himself.

We hear about the wrath and terrible judgment of of God, but in Jesus' four stories of the lost, you see none of that. The shepherd goes out into the night without complaint, and when he finds his sheep, he does not beat or scold. Instead, he says, "Rejoice with me; for I have found my sheep which was lost." Likewise, the woman diligently searches for her coin and she, too, rejoices over finding it. The father of the prodigal ran out to meet his returning son "and fell on his neck, and kissed him." The father was grieved because his other son chose to remain in the darkness. The door was not closed against him, he just refused to go in. Christ never got mad at the lost.

CHRIST SAVES THE LOST

How does Christ save the lost? With all of our theological terms we have made it sound so mysterious and supernatural. Go back and read the four Gospels and you see Jesus as a very lovable person. He taught and inspired people, He laughed and played with little children, He loved birds and flowers. He lived in such a way that people liked to be around Him. He talked to people about ordinary things of their lives—about the farmer plowing in the field, the woman cooking in the kitchen, about patched clothes, and He understood the day by day problems and cares of human life.

He sought to be the friend of all who would let him. There was Matthew, a greedy tax-collector; James and John who were simple fishermen; Mary and Martha, who were housekeepers; the woman at the well who was really a woman of the street. And gradually as they became His friends their lives were changed. As people associated with Him they became different.

As you read the record of His life on earth, you do not feel He was a weak, sentimental, unreal person. There was a tenderness about Him, yet there was also steel in Him. He laughed, but He was also stern. He loved, but He never compromised. As ordinary men and women came in contact with Him, they would begin to think about living in an extraordinary way. They would begin to be ashamed of sin and of cheap living. Some refused His friendship, others were unwilling to make the changes that friendship with Christ required. But a few stayed close to Him and gradually began to think as He thought. They never became perfect as He was, but they set Him as their goal and headed in His direction.

The New Testament tells us that after He died, He rose again and that He continued to live and is living among us today. Jesus Christ is alive! When the great truth takes possession of a person today, the process of salvation has begun. It means that we, too, can enter His transforming friendship. We may turn our backs upon Him and refuse His presence, but when one becomes His friend, then a lost one becomes found.

The main thing is to discover for yourself how friendship with Christ can become real. Reading the record of His days upon earth is a help. I have said to many, "Read thoughtfully and carefully the Gospel of Matthew ten times, and it will change your life," and many who have tried it have found it to be a marvelous experience. Regular worship in God's house has been the path that has led many to companionship with Him. As some have seen the Christ-likeness of certain people they have come to love the Christ.

There are many roads that lead to Christ. The Christian is not one who has gone all the way with Christ. None of us have. The Christian is one who has found the right road. Though you may not be at the end of your journey, if you are on the right road, at least your wandering has ceased. Even though you may not be home, if you know the way you are not lost. As I see it, a Christian is one who has become the friend of Christ and is ever seeking to cultivate that friendship.

Don't judge Christ by some person who is very unlike Him. Don't let the faults of some member of the church hide Christ from you. Forget for a moment the silly quarrels between the imperfect branches of His Church. Don't wait until you understand all the creeds and the things which have been said about Him. Don't hold back because you are conscious of some wrong in your life. Instead, imagine yourself alone with Jesus.

Talk to Him just as you would if He were with you in the flesh. Pour out your heart to Him fully realizing He will understand completely. Then listen as He talks to you. How does He tell you He wants you to live? What are the things in your life He would like to change? What spirit in your heart does He find that should not be there? What are the things He would like you to do? He will listen as you talk and He wants you to listen as He talks. Friendship requires that.

As He said to one, "Neither do I condemn thee, go. . . ." He forgets the past, He gives direction and purpose for the future, and above all we have His assurance, "Lo, I am with you." No wonder that one of the favorite songs of all Christians is, "What a Friend We Have in Jesus."

THE CHURCH AND THE LOST

Not only does Jesus describe those who are lost as He tells us about the sheep, coin and two sons, He also makes clear a perfect three-way program of evangelism for the Church. (1) There was the shepherd who went out to find the sheep. Though ninety-nine were safe in the fold, he could not rest as long as one was outside. In every community there are many people who could be won to Christ and the Church if some sincere and tactful person would take the time and effort to go to see them.

One thing we have demonstrated in America is that people can be sold. We sell insurance, washing machines, brushes, magazines and everything else. We can also sell Christ and His Church when we go out and try. I do not recall Jesus commanding us to attend church. He went Himself and gave us an example. But He specifically commanded His followers to go find others. He said, "Go out into the highways and hedges, and compel them to come in, that my house may be filled" (Luke 14:23). (2) The lost coin had not gone anywhere. Though it was lost, it was still in the house. The second type of evangelism for the Church is keeping up with the members it has. Go over the roll of a church and you find the names of many people who have ceased to support their church with either their presence, their gifts or their service.

Some of these get lost because they move from one place to another. When they move, they carry their furniture and nearly everything they have but their Church membership. Some get lost through loss of interest, or through the press of other interests. Some quit because their feelings get hurt. It is the business of the Church to keep up with its members. (3) A third type of evangelism is represented by the father of the prodigal. He did not go after the boy, but he maintained such an attractive home that the boy wanted to come back. In the far country he said, "I perish with hunger." He knew there was bread in his father's house.

There are a lot of people whose souls and hearts are hungry, and it is the business of the Church to maintain a program that will satisfy the needs of those who come. It is a supreme tragedy for a seeking soul to come to a church and find nothing there. We are not in danger of emphasizing too much the "going after" the lost, but we must be careful to provide the bread of life for those who come to the Father's House.

In each of these three stories, we note that Jesus deals with individuals. It was one sheep, not a flock. People are won to God, not in masses but one by one. It has been well said, "Winning people one at a time is the best way of winning the world, in time."

3. HOW TO LOSE AND FIND GOD

The Parable of the Prodigal Son

LUKE 15:11-24

THE FIRST SERMON I EVER TRIED TO PREACH WAS ABOUT the Prodigal Son. Through the years I have studied that story again and again, and I have preached no less than a hundred times on it. Each time I read the story I find something new, and I love it a little more. I used to think that a prodigal was one with a life wasted by wrong living who was a disgrace to himself, his family and his community. That may be true. On the other hand, there are many prodigals who have been very successful in life, who have achieved much and who are admired by many.

TO LIVE AS HE PLEASES

Let's look again at the story. There are four main points to emphasize. First, "Give me the portion of goods that falleth to me . . . the younger son gathered all together and took his journey." He decided that he could take the resources which were his, go his own way and live a better life. To remain at home meant to be subject to the will of his father. He wanted to be free.

To every person God gives certain abilities, opportunities and material possessions. God would like us to use what we have as His stewards, for us to live according to His will and way. God thinks that by living under His direction we will accomplish more. However, any one of us is at perfect liberty to take what we have and strike out on our own.

Notice the father did not deny that the boy had the right to claim his possessions, and neither did the father attempt to hold the boy at home. If the father had said, "No, I compel you to stay here under my will," then home would have ceased to be home. Instead it would have become a jail. He would have ceased to be a father and the son would have become a prisoner.

Why do people leave God out of their lives? It isn't because one is an atheist who does not believe. We can believe in God's existence and still ignore Him. Men do not leave God because they hate Him. People leave God because they do not feel that they need Him. They have resources sufficient, they can make their own laws and decide their own roads to travel. The prodigal is not necessarily one who wants to do wrong. The prodigal is one who feels sufficient with his own resources.

TO BE IN WANT

Notice the second point; "He began to be in want." In Jesus' story the boy spent all his money and began to want for material things. His clothes became threadbare, he had no place to live, he was compelled to eat

the food of the hogs. I have had many such come to
my study seeking a meal or a few dollars. On the other
hand, I have had just as many prodigals come to see me
who drove expensive cars, lived in fine houses and had
money to buy whatever they desired.

The boy did not leave home because he wanted to
hurt his father. He left because he felt he could work
out for himself a more satisfying life. But he was disappointed. Ask yourself if you have found in life what
you really want.

No person ever really seeks God as long as he feels
self-sufficient. It was a great hour in the life of the
Prodigal Son when he began to "perish with hunger."
It delights the heart of a mother to see her child eat
heartily at meal time. For a child to grow strong and
remain healthy, it needs good food. So God made the
child with an appetite. However, a lollipop eaten just
before dinner can spoil the child's appetite and prevent
its normal hunger from seeking the food which really
satisfies.

We were created with an instinctive hunger for
God. But it is possible to satisfy that hunger with lolli-
pops. Some people are satisfied with so little. The Prodigal Son took what his father gave him and lived as he
pleased. For a time no doubt he was happy. But one day
he realized "he had spent all." The fact that this particular prodigal had spent all his money is not the point.
I know prodigals who have plenty of money and material things, yet they have spent all.

This boy spent his conscience and in return he received a sense of guilt and shame. He spent the fellow-

ship of his father. Most surprising, he spent his freedom. The reason he left home in the first place was to be able to live his own life as he pleased. But later on "he went and joined himself to a citizen of that country; and he sent him into his fields to feed swine." Note the word "sent." The man who lives to do as he likes becomes the slave of his likes.

He came to the place where living was not the thrilling, zestful experience he thought it would be. Instead it was drudgery. His life was taken up doing a job that he hated. It was a great blessing to him that he came to that place because he was forced to look himself squarely in the face. So many people never really take stock of themselves. They satisfy the hungers of their hearts with frivolous things, and they keep rushing along and finally die in the chase, never finding in life the things that really count.

HE CAME TO HIMSELF

First, he decided he could manage his own life. Second, he began to be in want. Third, "he came to himself." That is wonderful. No one of us is a single self. Life would be so much simpler if we were. There is our careless self, which drifts along without thinking or trying. There is our passionate self. We do many things as a result of fear, anger, lust or some other passion. There is our greedy self. We can forget our obligations, we kill all the love in our hearts, if we let greed have its way. But, thank God, there is also our best self. "To thine own self be true."

A lot of people are not "at themselves." Sometimes

a deep sorrow, a set-back, a severe illness, or some other circumstance in life will bring us to our best selves. Some people never look up until they are on their backs. On the other hand, it is possible to go through life without ever really coming to your senses.

The Prodigal Son realized he had made a sorry mess of his life. He had not found what he wanted. The deep desires of his soul were not satisfied. He decides he cannot go it alone. No person becomes his best self by himself.

HE CAME TO HIS FATHER

Fourth, when the Prodigal Son comes to himself, he says, "I will arise and go to my father." In his situation, some people say "I will turn over a new leaf. I will do better." Some say, "I will become active in the church. I will make my life count for more." Those things are good but not good enough. That boy realizes he does not have the strength within himself. And blessed is that person who will settle for nothing less than the Father.

Notice the fact that the father did not go after the boy while he was in the far country. Just as he freely let him take what he had and leave him so the father lets the boy stay away until he decides he wants to come back. Our relationship with God is one of love and love cannot be compelled. For God to bring one of us back by force would destroy the relationship He wants. We are His sons, not His prisoners.

As the Prodigal comes back he says, "Father, I have sinned." He doesn't try to excuse himself. He blames nobody else. He doesn't make light of what he has done. Sometimes we say flippantly, "I don't claim to be perfect." But as long as we are flippant about it, God is forever beyond our reach. Sin is so serious that Jesus died because of it. The father said of the Prodigal, "This, my son was dead." Sin is as serious as death.

Not only did he come back to the father repenting of his sins, he also said, "Make me." He left his father saying, "Give me." His philosophy of life was to get what he could and do with it as he pleased. The road back to the father is the realization of self-failure and faith in His power. The boy also speaks of being a servant. "Make me as one of thy hired servants," he says. No Prodigal ever finds God until he is willing to yield himself completely. Not what I want to do, but what God wants me to do is the way back home.

What attitude does the father take toward his shabby, failing son? "When he was yet a great way off, his father saw him and had contempt, and went in the house, slammed the door and would not let the boy in." Is that the way the story reads? Or, "When he came home the father lectured and humiliated the boy and put him on probation." No. No. No. His father "had compassion, and ran, and fell on his neck, and kissed him."

The boy started his repentance, but the father did not even let him finish it. The spirit in his heart was enough. He had the servant to bring the best robe—the signs of the far country on the boy's body must be covered up. God not only forgives, He forgets. The Prodigal could sing with the Psalmist, "Blessed is he whose transgression is forgiven, whose sin is covered" (32:1).

"Put a ring on his hand, and shoes on his feet," the father commands. The ring signified membership in the family. Slaves went barefoot, but this was a son so he must have shoes. And the father says rejoicing, "My son is alive again." To come back to God means to begin living again.

4. THE MOST HOPELESS SINNER

The Parable of the Elder Brother
LUKE 15:11-32

MOST OF US HAVE RATHER VIVID RECOLLECTIONS OF RE-
vival meetings when some fiery evangelist would preach
"fearlessly" against sin. In thunderous tones he talked
about drinking and gambling, card playing and profanity
and all the sins of the flesh. He would tell about the
terrible hell that such sinners were going to, and he
would use high pressure methods to get the sinners to
hit the "sawdust trail." Occasionally some sinner would
be converted with blessed results. But usually such a
revival left the church and the community worse off.

It is true that there were people who committed
those sins. But they were not the only sinners. In fact
they were not the worst sinners. And such preaching not
only failed to save those who needed saving the most,
it made them more complacent and self-satisfied. The
hardest people to reach with the love of God are not
the bad people. They know they are bad. They have
no defense. The hardest ones to win for God are the
self-righteous people.

Some people criticized Jesus for associating with sin-

ners. So he told them a story about a father who had
two sons. One of these sons became a prodigal. He went
to the "far country." He wasted both his money and
his life. He sank to the level of a hog. The other of those
sons lived a decent, respectable life. As far as we know
he was never guilty of any immorality. To his father
he was able to say, "Neither transgressed I at any time
thy commandments."

Not only did he maintain his moral standards, he
was a hard worker. In fact, Jesus introduces him by
saying, "Now his elder son was in the field." Work is
good and is pleasing unto God. One of the world's
greatest paintings is *The Angelus* by Millet. The word
"angelus" means a prayer and that picture is of two
people praying in the field. On the horizon is the church
steeple and we presume the bell is ringing a call to
prayer. To understand the true significance of the picture, however, you must study where the rays of the
afternoon sun fall. They are not on the bowed heads
of the man and woman, neither do the rays fall on the
church steeple. They fall on the wheelbarrow and the
common tools. It is the artist's tribute to the dignity of
work.

There were the two boys. One who committed all
the sins which seem so wrong. The other who worked
hard and lived a decent life. Jesus' story ends with a
great banquet in the father's house. One of those boys
was seated at the table. He wore a new robe which his
father had given him. On his finger was the ring signify-
ing membership in the family. There was joy in his
heart. The other boy was out in the darkness, unhappy

and bitter, away from his father and the banquet table.

Now which boy was where? It was the "good" boy who was out in the dark at the end. Certainly Jesus is not telling us that we should commit the sins of the flesh. But He is pointing out that one can shut God out of his heart by "works," even good works. It is so easy to feel self-righteous and feel no need of the Father. That is the most dangerous sin.

THE SELF-SATISFIED PEOPLE

The people who gave Jesus the most trouble were not the so-called "sinners." They came to hear Him preach and from His lips they received not one word of condemnation. Jesus would take even a harlot and set her soul to singing. Surely there was a thrill in His voice as He described how, when the father saw his prodigal son returning, he "had compassion, and ran, and fell on his neck and kissed him." Jesus was accused of being "a friend of publicans and sinners" (Matthew 11:19). That he did not deny. His ministry was on their behalf. He said, "I came not to call the righteous but sinners to repentance" (Mark 2:17).

Those self-satisfied people in Christ's day and in our day are the most hopeless. The elder brother of the prodigal son never sank into the gutter. Instead, he stayed at home and worked and lived a moral life. As a result he began to build up within himself a sense of moral superiority. He began to pat himself on the back and feel he was better than his brother. The worse his brother became, the more self-righteous it made him feel.

It did not worry the elder son when his brother left the father's house and headed in the wrong direction. He never spent a sleepless night over the wrong of another. He never spent an hour in prayer for his brother's salvation. The father's heart was grieved and broken because of his boy, and he kept watching and eagerly hoping for his return. When the prodigal did return, the father welcomed him with a banquet. But the elder brother "was angry, and would not go in."

Here we see one of the greatest of all human sins, which is envy. Sometimes we get envy and jealousy confused with each other. Jealousy is not bad. In fact, it is normal and right. The Bible tells us that God is jealous (Exodus 20:5). Jealousy comes from love and when love is cheated, it has a right to be jealous. Any person is jealous for that which it loves, and if one has the right to love, he or she also has the right to be jealous.

But envy is a result of selfishness. St. Paul tells us, "Love envieth not" (1 Cor. 13:4). The envious person is always unhappy over the good fortune of another. It was envy that caused the first murder on earth. It was envy which nailed our Christ to the cross. "For he knew that for envy they had delivered him" (Matthew 27:18).

Because the boy would not come into the house, his father went out and entreated him. But notice the boy's reply, "Lo, these many years do I serve thee, neither transgressed I at any time thy commandment; and yet thou never gavest me a kid, that I mightest make merry with my friends." There he reveals his true motives. Why did he stay at home and work? Because he loved the father? No. Because of what he could get out of it.

We do not have to serve God in order to gain His material blessings. He gives us these anyway. It rains on the just and the unjust. God allows all of us the benefits of His good earth. But there is something to be gained from the Father far more wonderful. It is His fellowship.

DON'T MISS THE FELLOWSHIP

When I was in college my father used to write to me every week. I don't remember much that he wrote. In fact, I did not read his letters very carefully. Inside the letter would be a dollar, sometimes two, and that was what I was most interested in at that time. But since he died I have not seen nor heard from him. It seems that I think about him and miss him more each passing year. It isn't the dollar that I want. I miss him. There have been many problems I would like to have talked with him about. Some good things have happened to me that I wish I could tell him about.

Thinking about him, I begin to think about my Heavenly Father; I realize that sometimes I just take Him for granted. I gladly receive the material blessings that He sends my way, and often I become so absorbed in what He sends that I forget about what He says. But suppose tonight I realized that any communication between God and me was cut off. Suppose I could never feel His spirit again? Suppose I could never pray again? Why does a man marry? Is it to get someone to cook his meals, make the bed and sweep the floor? No, a man marries because he wants a wife. He could hire a housekeeper. Does a woman marry just to get someone to support her? No, she wants a husband. One of the saddest stories I know came out of the life of George F. Baker, the great banker. He was being given a testimonial dinner. Important bankers had come to pay him honor. Finally he rose to say a few words. He said, "Gentlemen, I appreciate what you have done for me tonight. But it doesn't mean much to me now. My wife died last year and I have no one to tell it to." Someone to tell it to. That means everything.

The other day I was in Mississippi for a few days. My brother, Stanley, drove a hundred miles to spend a night with me. We didn't have anything especially to talk about. Neither of us expected to get anything from the other. We just wanted to be together. If I needed it, he would give what money he had. If he needed it, I would give him what money I have. But that is the least, the very least thing in brotherhood. Being with one you love and who loves you means so much more.

Jesus told a story about two sons. One of those boys started out saying, "Give me." He did a lot of things which were bad and became a prodigal. But happily he "came to himself." He realized there is something better than material things. He found out there was something more satisfying than selfish pleasures. "I will arise and go to my father," he said.

But that elder brother never thought beyond himself. The father says to him, "This thy brother," but he will not accept that. He says, "This thy son." He missed knowing what it meant to really love and be loved. He complains to the father, "I have served you, but I have never received anything for it." Gently the father reminds him, "Thou art ever with me," but the boy can see none of the blessings of fellowship with his father.

The elder brother who worked and lived according to his father's laws only because he thought it would pay, ended up by ceasing to be a son and becoming merely a drudge and a slave. O the tragedy of one who lets love die within his heart. That is the lost person.

5. PRAY BECAUSE OF YOUR NEED

*The Parable of the Pharisee
and the Publican*

LUKE 18:9-14

THERE IS A STORY WHICH BEGINS: "TWO MEN WENT UP into the temple to pray." I like that. People go to the church for many different reasons. Some go to hear the sermon. Some go to hear the music and maybe to sing themselves. Some go to be with other people. Some go because as children they were carried and they got the church-going habit. Some go because they feel the church is an essential institution in the community and they know that if people did not attend the services the church would die. So they go because they want the church to live.

But the main reason for going to church is to pray. The fact is, prayer is the church's supreme business. Jesus said, "My house shall be called the house of prayer" (Matt. 21:13). The most important part of the church is not the pulpit, not the choir loft, not the social hall, it is the altar.

As the Bible tells about the building of the first churches, it is the altar that is emphasized. "And Noah

built an altar unto the Lord" (Gen. 8:20). "And there
Abraham builded an altar unto the Lord" (Gen. 12:7).
"And God said unto Jacob, Arise, go up to Bethel . . .
and make there an altar unto God" (Gen. 35:1). "And
Moses built an altar" (Exodus 17:15).

Every Sunday night as I watch hundreds of people
walk down the aisles of the church and kneel at the
altar to pray, I know that is the supreme moment. The
hymns have been sung, the sermon preached, and now
the worshiper is on his knees at God's altar, the most
sacred spot on earth. I never feel quite so definitely the
presence of God as I do then. As someone has written:

> No one has ever seen the wind,
> Neither you nor I.
> But when trees are bowing down,
> We know the wind is passing by.

> No one has ever seen God,
> Neither you nor I.
> But when heads are bowing down,
> We know the Lord is passing by.

Some go to the altar to confess and ask God's forgiveness. Some go to ask God's strength for a special
need. Some go to ask God's guidance. Some go to pray
for certain other people. Many go to thank God for His
blessings. In fact, no two pray exactly the same prayer,
but all need to pray some prayer. Every person is
"standing in the need of prayer."

"Two men went up into the temple to pray." Of
course, one can pray anywhere—kneeling at his bed-

side, walking down the street, while washing the dishes —but there is no place one can pray as effectively as kneeling in "the house of prayer." There we have the place, the atmosphere, the guidance and the inspiration.

One of the men was an outstanding citizen, known and respected. He probably was both financially and socially prominent. The other was an outcast, with no standing in the community. Yet, both went to the same church. I like that. In talking to me about coming to their church as pastor, some men said, "Ours is the most fashionable church in the city." That is not for me. I want a church that opens its doors to all who feel the need of God and bids each welcome. I think that is the kind Christ would have.

But one of these men failed in prayer. The other succeeded.

ONE MAN FAILED

One of the men wasted his time because his prayer utterly failed. He was not a bad man. In fact, he was a very fine man. He went to church, he observed the religious customs of his day, he gave a tithe of his income and, no doubt, he lived an upright life. But in spite of all his good points, God refused to hear his prayer.

What was the reason for his failure? He did not feel the need of God. He was conceited. He failed to hear Jesus say: "Blessed are the poor in spirit . . . they that mourn . . . which do hunger and thirst after righteousness" (Matt. 5:3-6). The truth is he did not look to God at all. Instead, he did what a lot of people do today, he picked out a few of his fellowmen who had failed and compared himself to them, saying, "God, I thank thee, that I am not as other men are." That man was not praying, he was just bragging. Clovis Chappell points out that he had a good eye on himself, a bad eye on his fellows, and no eye at all on God.

Above and beyond all things, real prayer comes from our sense of need. If you are as good as you want to be, then don't waste your time praying. I suggested to a man the other day that he pray and he replied, "I'm not fit to talk to God." I told him that is the most wonderful thing he could say. Then I quoted a verse to him:

> Let not conscience make you linger,
> Nor of fitness fondly dream.
> All the fitness He requireth,
> Is to feel the need of Him.

I think of at least three reasons why it is wrong to pick out some fellow who has not done as well as you and feel superior to him.

(1) You may be wrong because that fellow may be doing a lot better than you. God judges in the light of all the circumstances of one's life. Maybe, when everything is considered, that fellow is doing far better than you are. Jesus warns: "With what judgment ye judge, ye shall be judged" (Matt. 7:2). Be careful how you look at others.

(2) Comparing yourself with someone who seemingly has not done as well as you, makes you conceited. Conceit is the most fatal of all spiritual diseases. When you go to the doctor he will ask, "How is your appetite?" He knows that if you lose your appetite, you will not

eat properly and your body will waste away. Conceit kills one's spiritual appetite. It will cause one to cease to feed his soul and eventually he will die spiritually.

(3) The main reason it is wrong to compare ourselves with some less fortunate person is, it is an insult to God. We remember how Richard Baxter, as he watched some poor wretch go off to prison said, "There but for the grace of God, go I." Maybe God gave you more talents and better opportunities. Maybe He has poured His blessings more freely upon you. The very fact that you are getting along better than somebody else should drive you to your knees in thanksgiving.

If you feel any conceit, it is because you have been looking down. A mountain shames a molehill until both are humbled by the stars. Look up to God.

ONE MAN SUCCEEDED

The other man who went to church to pray went home "justified." That means all of his sins were wiped away, that a right relationship with God was restored. Nothing is more wonderful than to be justified by God. It means the burdens of the conscience are lifted, our haunting fears are driven out, we are given new freedom —happiness—peace.

That man's prayer was a great success. I want to find out more about it. As I read the story I find he was an outcast. That is encouraging. It indicates that no matter who you are or what you have done, you still have God's permission to come into His presence and talk to Him.

In my imagination I meet that man (it might have

been a woman) on his way to the church. As the pastor of a church on a main thoroughfare of a big city, I have come to know many just like him. As we meet I ask, "Where are you going?" "To the church," he says. I am surprised so I reply, "I didn't think you belonged to any church. At any rate I know you have not been attending." "No," he answers, "I have neglected the church, but I've reached the place where I need help. Every other source has failed me and now I am going to God."

I see he is in dead earnest, and there is no sight more thrilling than to see such a one moving toward the secret place of the most high. I turn and follow him and as we walk along I find myself humming the familiar hymn:

Just as I am, without one plea,
But that thy blood was shed for me.
And that thou bidd'st me come to Thee;
O Lamb of God, I come. I come.

When he goes to the altar to pray, I get as close as possible. I have no right to listen to his prayer. It is a private matter between him and his Lord, but I am interested and want to hear it. I know something of the shoddy way he has lived, and I expect to hear him telling God about the tough breaks he had, about the wrong crowd that influenced him, and all the other excuses he can think of. I get myself set for a long prayer. Instead, his prayer is short, just seven words. He simply prays, "God be merciful to me, a sinner."

That is all. That is enough. He really prayed those words. And Jesus said he went back home that day

"justified." As we move out of the church, I begin
singing, "Happy day, happy day, when Jesus washed
my sins away." Nothing is grander than that.

There is a little book, *Beside the Bonnie Brier Bush.*
It tells about Dr. MacLure, a faithful minister of Christ
for forty years. He had reached the end of the way and
sent for a friend to read the Bible to him. The friend
began reading, "In my Father's house are many mansions . . ." but the old preacher stopped him.

"That is too good for me," he said. Instead, he had
his friend turn to Luke 18 and read: "And the publican,
standing afar off, would not lift up so much as his eyes
unto heaven, but smote upon his breast, saying, God be
merciful to me a sinner."

6. PRAY UNTIL YOU GET THE ANSWER

The Parable of the Friend at Midnight
LUKE 11:5-13

THIS QUESTION CAME TO ME: "JESUS SAID, 'ASK AND IT shall be given thee.' How many times should I pray for something?" Jesus answered that question with a story about a man who had an unexpected guest at midnight. Custom required that he serve his guest but, as it was with "Old Mother Hubbard," his cupboard was bare.

Being midnight, there were no stores open where he could buy some food. So he goes over and begins knocking on his neighbor's door. From inside comes a sleepy voice saying, "Trouble me not: the door is now shut, and my children are with me in bed; I cannot rise and give to thee."

I sympathize with the neighbor. It was dark and he had no convenient light switch as we have. To make a light was considerable trouble. The fire was out, and it is never pleasant to get out of a warm bed in a cold house. And doubtless he had had trouble getting the children to sleep. If he got up, likely they would awaken and it would be a problem getting them back to sleep.

The man, however, keeps on knocking and finally

his neighbor gets up and gives to him, "because of his importunity," said Jesus. "Importunity" means persistence, to keep on. Then to this story Jesus adds, "Ask, and it shall be given you; seek, and ye shall find; knock, and it shall be opened unto you."

Jesus does not mean that God is like the reluctant neighbor. Instead, what He would have us understand is that, if a man would answer a request merely to keep from being bothered further, how much more will God answer our requests of Him. But the secret of power in prayer is persistence.

We make frequent requests of God, but before our requests become real prayers we must, even as the friend at midnight, come in the spirit of urgent need. We must remember that Heaven only hears what we are determined it shall hear. God is not a trifler, He is completely in earnest, and He does not hear us until we become tireless in our determination.

We remember how Jacob wrestled with his "angel" saying, "I will not let thee go, except thou bless me" (Genesis 32:26). Jesus told his disciples, ". . . tarry ye in the city of Jerusalem, until ye be endued with power from on high" (Luke 24:49). Note the words: "tarry" —"until." Before Paul received the grace sufficient for the thorn in his flesh, he prayed three times (11 Cor. 12:8). For other things he might have prayed three hundred times because he tells us he prayed "without ceasing" (Romans 1:9). Jesus prayed until, "His sweat was as it were great drops of blood falling down to the ground" (Luke 22:44).

How many times should I pray for something?

Until the answer comes! As our fathers used to say, "Until you pray it through."

PRAYER CHANGES THINGS—EVEN YOU

But a mother says to me, "When my boy went away to the battlefield, I prayed that God would keep him safe. I was persistent in my praying, not just once did I ask or just once a day. It was my constant prayer all day long every day. But he was killed. I asked, but God did not answer."

My reply is that God did hear her prayer and that He did have the power to keep her boy safe. God could change the course of bullets in their flight, if He chose to. God answers prayer. So obviously, the keeping of that boy safe was not His answer. The thing this mother must do is to keep on praying until she does get God's answer. God answers at the proper time in the proper way, and it is not ours to question how and when, it is ours to pray until the answer comes.

Jesus tells us that "men ought always to pray, and not to faint" (Luke 18:1). To faint means to quit. One can allow bitterness, or disappointment, or lack of understanding, or hopelessness to turn him away from God. And though God's answer may be better than anything we had dreamed of, because we have turned from Him, we fail to get that answer and thereby miss the supreme blessing of life for us.

Persistent prayer does two things: it changes the course of events, and second, it changes us. Our world is not a rigid, fixed, mechanical thing. It is a spiritual universe, governed by powerful forces far beyond the present understanding of mankind. Jesus so understood the governing forces of the world that He could speak to the winds and waves and they obeyed His voice. He could heal sickness in a moment's flash, He could make the blind see, the cripple walk, even the dead live.

Certainly we do not understand the higher spiritual forces which have the power to change even our physical world. But we do not have to understand this power to use it. We do not know what electricity is, where it comes from or how it is made. But nevertheless, we use it to light up our homes, run our factories, and in a thousand other ways. Marconi, who invented the wireless, told a friend that there was one thing he did not understand about it and that was "why it works."

Scientists told us about atomic power. Because we believed that power existed and that it could be harnessed, we spent millions of dollars to develop it. Some day that power will heat our homes, run our automobiles and serve mankind in so many ways.

Scientists are also telling us about spiritual power. Steinmetz said, "The greatest discoveries in the next fifty years will be in the realm of the spiritual." We hear Dr. J. B. Rhine saying, "As a result of thousands of experimental trials we found it to be a fact that the mind has a force that can act on matter." And when the mind of man meets the mind of God through the medium of prayer something happens. Prayer changes things. So, instead of fainting, we keep on praying until the change does come.

"NO" IS NOT AN ANSWER

Jesus tells us, ". . . your Father knoweth what things ye have need of, before ye ask him" (Matt. 6:8).

So why should we persistently keep on asking Him? Because frequently God's answer must be delayed until we are ready to receive it. Not only does persistent prayer set in motion spiritual forces in our world, also it works changes within ourselves.

Mrs. Browning tells us, "Every wish, with God, is a prayer," but frequently our wishes need to be cleansed and purified. It is true that God "knoweth what things we have need of," but it is just as true that often we ourselves do not know. We just think we know and mercifully God withholds an answer until we come with the right request. It is often said that "No" is an answer, but "No" is never the final answer. God has a glorious "Yes," and we must keep on asking until that "Yes" comes. To merely accept God's "No" is to accept defeat.

Paul asked God for the chance to preach in Bythinia. God said "No," but Paul kept on asking until he got a "Yes." The "Yes" was to go into Macedonia. There Paul did his greatest work. If he had stopped on the "No," we would never have heard of him. Edison received a thousand "No" answers to his prayers for the secret of the light bulb. But he kept on until the "Yes" came.

If God says "No" to our prayer, it does not mean we should stop praying. It means that we keep praying until we find the prayer to which He can say "Yes." The supreme object of prayer is not the attainment of some desire, but rather is it to know God. Knowing God, we know His purposes and knowing His purposes, we desire them above our own. And desiring His purposes, it then becomes safe for God to entrust us

with His power. But God will not give us His power for
unworthy uses.

Read again the story of Jacob's prayer. If God will
do what he asks and will give him what he wants, then
he promises to support God's work and give him a tenth
of his income (Genesis 28:20-22). That is mere child-
ish bargaining, yet we pray the same way. "Lord, if you
will make me well I will go to church." "If you will
look after my son on the battlefield, I will live a good
life." "If you will help me to get more money, I will
give you a tithe." To that sort of praying God says
"No."

Jacob kept on praying and one morning after
wrestling all night with God in prayer, he prayed, "Tell
me, I pray thee, thy name." To know a name was to
know the person. So Jacob's persistence led him to the
supreme prayer, "Reveal thyself to me." God answered
with a glorious "Yes." Jacob forgets the bargains he
wanted to make, he is not thinking of what he can get
out of God, but with humility and reverence, he says,
"I have seen God face to face."

Suppose you could go into a room where Jesus was
sitting. What would you do? Would you give him a
list of all the things you want, as children give to Santa
Claus? Would you ask him the explanation of a dozen
problems you have been unable to solve? No—you
would fall on your knees, you would kiss the hem of His
garment, and being with Him, all your desires would be
satisfied. That is where we get to when we keep on praying ' 'til we pray it through.'

7. YOUR PRAYER WILL BE ANSWERED

The Parable of the Friend at Midnight

LUKE 11:5-13

WE HAVE THE PROMISE OF GOD: "CALL UNTO ME, AND I will answer thee" (Jeremiah 33:3). Jesus emphasized the fact that God keeps that promise. He said, "Ask, and it shall be given you" (Matt. 7:7). He said, "All things, whatsoever ye shall ask in prayer, believing, ye shall receive" (Matt. 21:22). He said, "If two of you shall agree on earth as touching any thing that they shall ask, it shall be done for them of my Father" (Matt. 18:19).

Yet, right in the Bible we find many prayers that it seems God did not answer. Moses prayed to enter the Promised Land, but his request was refused and he died. The Psalmist said, "Oh my God, I cry in the daytime, but thou hearest not" (22:2). In Lamentations we read, "Thou covered thyself with a cloud, so that no prayer can pass through" (3:44). Habakkuk asks, "O Lord, how long shall I cry and thou wilt not hear" (1:2). St. Paul asked that a "thorn in the flesh" which handicapped his work be removed, but his prayer request was not granted (II Cor. 12:9). Even Christ prayed "Let this cup pass from me," but He drank its bitter dregs.

There are many people today who have lost faith because when they called unto God they seemed to receive no answer. They even felt that their prayers went unheard, that they were just speaking words out into space. Well, what is the answer for the problem of unanswered prayer?

The fault may be in us. We remember that Jesus warns us that if we refuse to forgive others, God will not forgive us (Matt. 6:15). And the Psalmist says, "If I regard iniquity in my heart, the Lord will not hear me" (66:18). James says, "Ye ask, and receive not because ye ask amiss" (James 4:3).

Because of our own refusal to do ourselves what we ask God to do, because of our refusal to face the sin of our own lives, because of asking for the wrong reasons, we do not get the answer we ask for. The first prayer, and the beginning of every prayer, should be "Search me, O God, and know my heart: try me and know my thoughts" (Psalm 139:23). God makes the sun to shine, but if the window in our house is dirty, God will not make the sun come through. The darkness in your room may not be a cause for asking God to make the sun shine brighter. Rather it may be a cause for you to wash your windows.

The darkness of your soul, and the littleness which you have received, the confusion in which you live, may not be because God has not answered, it may be because you are unwilling to receive. God has two kinds of gifts for us: first, there are the ones he gives whether we ask for them or not—the sun which shines, the air we breathe, the fertility in the soil. Parents give to their children such things as food, shelter, clothing and watchful care whether the child asks for it or not.

The other kind of gifts are given only if we ask for them. I want my son to have a college education, but I cannot give it to him unless he asks for it and wants it. If I make available for him the money he needs, he must cooperate by opening his mind through study in order to receive the education. Yes, the reason we do not receive the answers to our prayers may be in us.

THREE POSSIBLE ANSWERS

When we make a request to God through prayer, we must remember there are three possible answers we might receive. They are: yes, no, or wait.

Frequently God's answer to our prayers is an immediate "yes." Sometimes He must say "no." Jesus once said to a mother, "Ye know not what ye ask" (Matt. 20:22). My nine year old son has asked me repeatedly to buy him a rifle "that shoots real bullets." I think it is better for him, and I am sure it is better for the rest of the family and for our neighbors for me to say "no."

More often God says "no" in order to say "yes" to something better. At the end of my second year in college I sought to get a job teaching school. I did not have the money to go to college the next year, and I was almost desperate. The choice in one school was between me and another man and I prayed that they would elect me. Instead, they elected the other man and I felt God had refused to answer my prayer.

A little later I got a letter from Dr. Snyder at Wofford College opening the way for me to go there and I went. Now as I look back I see that God's "no" to my prayer was the best answer I could have received. I probably would have been a miserable failure as a school teacher, my college work was not interrupted, and the next summer the way was opened for me to enter the ministry, which was what I really wanted.

One of the greatest saints of all time was Augustine. He tells how his mother, Monica, went to the church and prayed all one night that God would not let him sail for Italy. He was a wild youth and she feared for him to come under the influence of the wicked city of Rome. She wanted to keep him near that she might lead him to Christ.

God said "no" to her prayer and refused to prevent Augustine from sailing. In Rome he went to hear the great Ambrose preach and he became a Christian. Later, Monica was glad God let her son go.

Nearly all of us have had the experience of praying for some person to be kept safe or to be made well and yet the person died. At such times there comes over us a feeling of being forsaken. Yet I am sure that the greatest blessing even God can give is the blessing of death. To deny one the privilege of dying is to deny the privilege of living with God in the Father's House.

I prayed recently for a young mother to live. Her two children needed her so badly, yet she died. Parents have prayed for their children and yet they died. Often we cannot understand why God says "no," but there will come a time when we will understand. As Paul said,

"For now we see through a glass darkly; but then face to face: now I know in part; but then shall I know even as also I am known" (1 Cor. 13:12).

Until our prayers are answered, we must have faith. Faith means trusting where we cannot see. If everything were completely clear to us, we would not need faith and whatever God's answer to our prayer is, we must remember "the judgments of the Lord are true and righteous altogether" (Psalm 19:9).

Frequently God's answer to our prayer is "wait." We remember how Jacob asked God for a favor and in return Jacob promised to give gifts to God. Later on, as Jacob wrestled with the angel, he forgot what he wanted God to do, instead he wanted God. He says, "I will not let thee go, except thou bless me" (Genesis 32:26). That night Jacob received the greatest blessing of his life. He says, "I have seen God face to face."

Too often we are so concerned about the gift that we forget to seek the giver, and God may withhold the things we pray for if those things might keep us from seeing Him. In fact, I think God may take away some of the things He has given already because we put those things before Him.

The asking for things and for favors from God is really the least important purpose of prayer. Jesus told His disciples to first pray "Our Father." Getting to know God is better than things we might ask for. The main object of prayer is to glorify Him. If you would learn to pray, study the Psalms. For the most part they are the prayers of a people in poverty, yet they almost never asked for things.

"Bless the Lord, O my soul; and all that is within me, bless his holy name"—"The Lord reigneth; let the earth rejoice"—"O give thanks unto the Lord; for he is good"—"Teach me, O Lord, the way of thy statutes; and I shall keep it unto the end. Give me understanding, and I shall keep thy law; yea, I shall observe it with my whole heart"—"Let the words of my mouth and the meditation of my heart be acceptable in thy sight, O Lord, my strength and my redeemer."

Praise, thanksgiving, consecration and communion —those are the prayers that bring the greatest blessings to our lives. It is not wrong to want things and to ask for them. God made everything there is. But the mere possession of things does not satisfy our souls. The removing from our hearts of selfish and unholy desires by the indwelling of His Spirit is a wonderful answer to prayer. As George Meredith, in his novel *The Ordeal of Richard Feverel*, said: "Who rises from prayer a better man, his prayer is answered."

Also, we must remember that part of the answer to our prayers must be made by us. Augustine said, "Without God, we cannot. Without us, God will not." God gives the wheat, but man must till the soil, sow, reap, grind into flour and bake, if he would eat the bread.

When the children of Israel came to the Red Sea, Moses goes apart to pray. In answer God said, "Speak unto the children of Israel, that they go forward" (Exodus 14:15). God is saying He has done all that He needs to do. Now they must do what they can do. Sometimes God's answer to us is wisdom sufficient to know what we should do, sometimes it is strength sufficient to walk, sometimes it is inspiration to cause us to use what He has already given us.

When the final record is written, God will see that no prayers were left unanswered.

8.   WHEN THE HEART IS HUNGRY

The Parable of the Great Supper
LUKE 14:15-24

TO ILLUSTRATE SOME VERY PROFOUND AND IMPORTANT truths, Jesus told a story about a man who prepared a great supper and invited a number of his friends to come and eat with him. However, instead of coming to the supper, those invited sent their excuses. So the man invited others who did come. The story ends with the host stating that none of those which were first invited shall taste of his supper.

As I read that story the first thing I think of is hunger. The reason for having a supper is to satisfy our hungers. There is the hunger of our physical bodies which has the power to drive us beyond all reason. Under the power of unsatisfied hungers, men can be changed into heartless beasts. The Bible tells of the siege of Samaria by Ben-hadad. Two mothers become so crazed with hunger that they made a compact to kill and eat first the baby of one and then of the other (2 Kings 6:27-29).

However, man's hunger goes beyond the animal level. Carlyle points out that man is the only animal that cooks his food. He wants his food not only to be satisfying but tasty and attractive. Just a shelter that keeps out the rain and protects against the cold is enough for a dog or a cow. But man is not satisfied with just shelter. He wants pictures on his walls and rugs on his floor. Just the fulfillment of animal desires is not sufficient for man.

Man hungers for beauty, for love, for a feeling of importance, for security. Far more important than his animal appetite, is the deep hunger of his heart. We agree with James Terry White:

> If thou of fortune be bereft,
> And in thy store there be but left
> Two loaves, sell one and with the dole,
> Buy hyacinths to feed thy soul.

There is an even greater hunger in man. "As the hart (deer) panteth after the water brooks, so panteth my soul after thee, O God" (Psalm 42:1). We hunger for God.

When we think of religion, we think of crosses and self-denials, of sacrifices and duties. We think it means turning away from all the things we like, putting a frown on our face and a burden on our backs. Jesus says finding God is like sitting down to a great supper. I am glad He used the word "supper." It always amuses me to see some fellow who grew up in the country move into town and start getting "high-hat." And one of the first signs is when he starts calling, "supper," "dinner."

When I think of supper, I think of the big kitchen we used to have with the long table and the bench across the back-side. When all seven of the children were at home, a bench was necessary. I think of how hungry we were and how good everything tasted. Did you ever crumble corn bread into a tall glass of cold milk? That would not be good manners at dinner but at supper it is wonderful.

To me supper means not only eating when you are hungry. It means being with those you love. It means laughter and joy and fellowship. It means satisfying not only the body, but also the heart. Jesus wants us to know that coming to God is like coming to supper.

EXCUSES AND REASONS

Jesus likens possessing God to the story of the man who made a great supper. Some that he invited refused the invitation and, instead, sent excuses. There is a vast difference between a reason and an excuse. An excuse is what we give when we do not want to do something and we do not have a reason. Look at the excuses the men gave in Jesus' story.

It was to a supper they were invited. When is a supper held? It is always at night. One man's excuse is, "I have bought a piece of ground, and I must needs go and see it." How could he look at his field in the dark? Another one says, "I have bought five yoke of oxen, and I go to prove them." It is almost impossible to plow oxen in the daytime, much less at night. Another man says, "I have married a wife." In this modern day of ours that would be a reason, but in that day women's position was so inferior to men's, then it was only an excuse.

Why do we make an excuse? It is because we realize

we are doing the wrong thing. I hear people give all sorts of excuses as to why they do not go to church—do not like the minister, people are unfriendly, the church is costing too much, the services are dull, some of the members are hypocrites, etc., etc. But never one time have I ever heard a person make an excuse for going to church. We do not make excuses for doing the right thing, our excuses are for doing the wrong thing.

A lady told me she did not go to church because she worked hard all the week and she needed to rest on Sundays. That was her excuse. Her reason, not her excuse, was that she felt no need of God. Most church services do not begin until eleven o'clock. And then there is the service on Sunday night. She could at least get rested by Sunday night. She went to her work because she needed the salary she earned to buy food, clothes, shelter and the necessities of life. She does not regard the worship of God as one of life's necessities, and that is her reason for not going to God's house. That resting idea is no reason.

An invitation even to a great supper has no appeal to one who is not hungry. And, though true fellowship with God is food for our souls, it does not interest those who have satisfied themselves with other things. If you do not want God and if you do not feel the need of God, then you are likely to make excuses instead of accepting God's invitation.

In Jesus' story there were others who did accept the invitation to the supper—"the poor, and the maimed, and the halt, and the blind." Those people had struck it hard and knew what privation meant. When warm fellowship and food was offered, they gladly came. Jesus gives us an invitation, never a subpoena. And we never accept His invitation until we have a reason.

If you refuse God, He will wait and one day weariness may toss you to His breast, maybe sometime you will realize the poverty in just possessing things, maybe your heart will be maimed, maybe you will not be able to walk by yourself, maybe the life for you will grow dark. Then you will be ready for the bread of life.

BE GLAD FOR YOUR HUNGER

The conclusion of the story is, "None of those men which were bidden shall taste my supper." It isn't that the host was angry at his neighbors and shut the door in their faces. Certainly God never withdraws His invitation to any person.

The old preachers used to quote: "As long as the lamp holds out to burn, the vilest sinner may return." That is true. No matter who you are or what you have done, His invitation to you is still open.

There is a legend that later on the night of the supper the three men, who made excuses and did not go, met and got to talking about it. "Maybe," one said, "we missed something." Their curiosity began to get the better of them so they decided to walk by the house of the supper on their way home. They looked through the window and saw a table laden with sumptuous food. It was later in the evening and they were hungrier than they were when their invitation came. They saw people in the lighted rooms who were happy. Out in the darkness they felt alone. So they went around to the door, but they were turned back. They had lost their chance.

I doubt that legend. What is more probable is the men whose excuses were "I have bought a piece of ground," "I have bought five yoke of oxen," "I have married a wife," became so absorbed with property, activity and social life, that they never thought of the invitation again. Certainly that happens again and again in those who refuse God's invitation to come to Him. We can deafen our ears to the voice of God so long that eventually we cease to hear His call. Such a one does not worry about it. In his spiritual deadness he becomes complacent and satisfied, and the riches of the kingdom of God go forever beyond his grasp.

On the other hand, if you feel your life has lost its meaning, then be glad. Many people once declared their freedom to do as they please. Religion spoke of consecration and stewardship so they passed it by. But sometimes one feels like the little girl who asked her mother, "What can I do today?" The mother replied, "Anything you want to." She answered, "But I am tired of doing what I want to do." Until one decides God's way is the best way, he never really prays, "Take my life and let it be, consecrated Lord to Thee."

If you still feel a hunger in your heart, be glad. Too many people can be satisfied with going to a show, or by getting drunk, or with the things that money can buy, or with a little applause from the crowd. Some people seem satisfied with so little. As long as your heart is still hungry, there is hope that you may give God a chance. Many people have been so enriched by Christ that they would rather give up anything they have rather than lose Him. He must be real. "Today if ye will hear his voice, harden not your hearts" (Psalm 95:7-8).

9. WHEN YOU ARE WOUNDED

The Parable of the Good Samaritan
LUKE 10:30-37

JESUS BEGINS A STORY WITH A MAN WALKING ALONG THE highway who fell among thieves and was left wounded. I have thought about that man a lot, but I know very little about him. I do not know his name, his race or his nationality. He may have been rich or poor, he may have been educated or ignorant, no one knows. Maybe he was an old man approaching the sunset of life, but he might have been young with most of his life ahead.

The fact is it could have been any person. It could be you because, regardless of who you are you can be wounded. A man was by to see me just last week. He told me that once he had a good job and a place of respect in the community, but he had lost out, and he wondered if I would help him. He was hungry, he had no place to sleep. Maybe his condition was his own fault, maybe it wasn't, but the fact remained that now he was by the roadside—wounded.

I met a lovely young girl the other day and noticed she was wearing an engagement ring. I asked, "When do you plan to get married?" She barely whispered, "He died last year." That girl is by the roadside—wounded. After a service the other night, a man and his wife waited to talk with me about the recent death of their only child. Without him their journey through life has lost much of its meaning. They, too, are by the roadside—wounded.

There is a dear friend in the hospital. His health has been overcome by a sickness that will leave him an invalid the balance of his days. He understands the fact that one can be left wounded. I need not name others. In so many ways we can be hurt. Often, it seems, when we are making our greatest progress and when life is for us at its best, suddenly some disaster breaks upon us and becomes a thief that takes away that which we loved so much and leaves us by the highway of life—wounded.

We might say, "It was the man's fault. He knew it was a dangerous road from Jerusalem down to Jericho so he should have stayed at home." Certainly we should take reasonable precaution. But on the other hand, there is no way to shelter yourself completely.

There was a story in the paper about a man who stayed at home one Fourth of July. He said it was too dangerous to be out on the highway. But as he was sitting in his backyard, a tin can fell out of an airplane and hit him on the head and severely hurt him. I know of a man who refused to fly in an airplane because he felt it was too dangerous. Yet one day he slipped in the bath tub and broke his neck. We might say the first man should not have been sitting out in the yard, but we hardly would want to say the other man should not have been taking a bath.

No, the fact is, life itself carries with it the possibility of being hurt. If a person had absolutely no feeling of any kind, he could not be hurt but a person without feeling is dead. So the fact that you can be wounded is a sign that you are alive.

The usual sermon on Jesus' story of the good Samaritan talks about thieves who rob and hurt others, about the priest and Levite who passed by a wounded man without helping, and about the Samaritan who did help. The sermons on this story remind us how we should respect the rights of others and how at all times we should be good Samaritans.

But there are times when we are in no position to be a good Samaritan. Instead, we find ourselves as the one wounded and left by the roadside. As the pastor of a church in a city, I have opportunity to minister to many wounded people. To them I try to say three things:

YOU ARE NOT KILLED

(1) To be wounded means you are not killed. That means you still have life and as long as there is life there is hope. So, the first step is to concentrate, not on our problems but on our possibilities. James Gordon Gilkey tells the story of the American submarine named the *Squalus*. One morning in May 1939 she went to sea to make some practice dives. Something went wrong and it plunged to the bottom in 240 feet of water. Of the fifty-nine men on board twenty-six were killed and the others barely escaped with their lives. What a dismal ending for that ship's career.

But that was not the end. The ship was salvaged and repaired and renamed the *Sailfish*. When the Second World War began, she was sent to the Pacific and the official story stated, "One night the *Sailfish* battled darkness, a typhoon, colossal waves and torrential rains to stalk and finally sink one of Japan's 22,000-ton aircraft-carriers . . . For this victory the Commander of the *Sailfish* was awarded the Navy Cross, and the *Sailfish* herself was given a Presidential Citation."

Think about that! The ship that lay disabled and helpless at the bottom of the sea, had now become one of the proudest of the fleet. We have been thrilled by the story of Ben Hogan. His car was hit by a heavy bus, and he lay wounded by the roadside. A great career in golf was ended, we thought. It was doubtful if he could ever walk again, but as soon as possible he got some braces and began to swing his golf clubs. It was painful, but he kept swinging and came back to win both the United States and the British championships.

The tragedy in life is not the wound because life is so constituted that the wound is inevitable. The tragedy comes when one quits instead of coming back. There are times when we must grit our teeth and say, "I may be down but I am not out." George Washington fought nine major battles. He lost six of the nine but he kept coming back until he won the war.

HELP WILL COME YOUR WAY

(2) When you are wounded, you can count on help coming your way. Often it is help you did not expect. As the man in Jesus' story lay by the roadside, it

must have been a disappointment to hear the footsteps of the priest and the Levite as they passed him by. He thought surely they would help.

Presently he heard other steps and this time they stopped by his side. It was a Samaritan, a man of an outcast, despised race. The Samaritans were treated so badly you could hardly expect any compassion from one of them. But tenderly the hurts of the wounded man were bound up, he was put upon the donkey and carried to safety. It usually works out like that. When we need it, we get help that we had not counted on.

On my office wall hangs Borthwick's painting, "The Presence." It shows a beautiful cathedral into which a penitent, burdened soul has come. Her clothes are shabby and obviously life for her has been hard. But she kneels in the church and the presence of Christ is there by her side. As I look at that painting, I recall how one day He stood in the little church of his home town and announced: "He hath sent me to heal the broken-hearted" (Luke 4:18). Not only do the wounded have the help of other people, they also have the help of God who is our Father.

The assurance of God's help gives serenity and power. Elizabeth Cheney puts it this way:

Said the Robin to the Sparrow:
"I would really like to know,
Why these anxious human beings,
Rush about and worry so."

Said the Sparrow to the Robin:
"Friend, I think that it must be,

That they have no Heavenly Father,
Such as cares for you and me."

DON'T BECOME BITTER

(3) Don't let your wounds make you bitter. Charles
M. Crowe tells how Louis B. Mayer, the movie man, got
into a fight once when he was a school boy and came out
second best. At home that night he muttered hateful
words against the other boy and vowed to get even. His
mother heard him but said nothing then. The next day
the Mayer family went on a picnic out in the mountains.
Louis' mother called him over to a little clearing that
faced a mountain wall. She told him to say what he said
last night. He was ashamed but she insisted and he said,
"Damn you." She told him to shout it like he had done.
He did, and from the mountains all around came his
words back to him saying, "Damn you."

Now his mother told him to shout, "Bless you."
He did, and the whole world seemed to be saying back
to him, "Bless you," as the echo of his voice came back.
Then she reminded him of the words of Christ: "Love
your enemies, bless them that curse you, do good to
them that hate you, and pray for them which despitefully
use you, and persecute you" (Matt. 5:44).

Louis Mayer understood and the law of the echo
became the law of his life.

10. THE FOUR PEOPLE WHO GO TO CHURCH

The Parable of the Four Soils

MATTHEW 13:3-23; MARK 4:2-20;
LUKE 8:4-15

THERE ARE FOUR TYPES OF PEOPLE WHO GO TO CHURCH. And the tragedy is that three out of the four receive no lasting good by going. The glory of it is that the life of one out of the four is supremely blessed. Whether one is helped by going to church depends not so much on the church or the preacher but upon himself. Jesus makes all this clear in a story He told about a farmer who went out to sow his seed.

The seed represents the word of God and the sower represents the church. I know that often we do a poor job at sowing the seed. To me is given the blessed privilege of preaching to large congregations twice each Sunday. As best I can, I read and think and write to make my sermons simple and easy to understand, to make them as winsome and effective as possible. And then I go home Sunday night humiliated because of the shoddy job I have done that day.

On the other hand, I remember there was one who spoke the words of eternal life as no man ever spoke. His was the most winsome voice the world has ever known and they nailed Him to a cross. Russell Lowell said, "Every man is a prisoner of his fate"; and we might add that every preacher is a prisoner of his congregation. The emphasis in Jesus' story is not on the seed, neither is it upon the sower, but rather the final determining factor is the soil upon which the seed falls. Look at the four soils and decide which type you are.

THE WAYSIDE

(1) Some seed fell "by the wayside." The wayside was a hardened path or roadway in which the seed could find no lodgment. In any congregation you find a lot of "wayside" people. For some every question has been settled, they do not want to be disturbed by any fresh ideas or new growth.

I remember well how I tried to get one of my first congregations to lift its eyes and do more to spread the Kingdom of God. As we approached the time when we would decide what we would give the following year, I did my best. I preached and prayed and talked to the people. But when the question came up at the conference, one man, who was the leader, spoke up and said, "I move we continue what we have been giving." His mind was completely closed to the thought of any progress. In my denomination the bishop moves the preacher. I think sometimes he ought to move the congregation and let the preacher stay.

There are those who are self-righteous and spiritually

complacent. They never realize the sermon is for them. They are thinking of the sins of somebody else and hoping the preacher will "pour it on 'em." We talk about "hardened sinners" but "hardened saints" are a lot harder.

Some people's hearts are hardened by a bitter disappointment. Some person they believed in failed to measure up and they refuse to believe ever again. Maybe some prayer was not answered as they expected, and they become embittered. By habitual thinking, self-righteousness, disappointment, sorrow and in many other ways our hearts become hardened. It always brings a tear to my eye to read the story of Felix. One day as he listened to Paul talk about the faith in Christ, Felix trembled. He felt a pull at his heart's door. But he said, "Go thy way for this time; when I have a more convenient season, I will call for thee" (Acts 24:25). But his heart never trembled again. Each refusal of God adds to the hardening crust around a heart.

STONY GROUND

(2) Some seed fell on "stony ground." Much of the land in Palestine was extremely rocky. The soil was rich, but it had no depth and though the grain would spring up quickly and give promise of a fine harvest, when the hot sun of the summer began to beat down, it would wither. There are a lot of "stony soil" people. They get very enthusiastic and excited about their religion. Now that much is good.

We sometimes refer to certain people as "religious fanatics." But I had rather try to restrain a fanatic than to resurrect a corpse. If some new spiritual stirring of your soul should bring a tear to your eye or a shout of praise to God in your voice, be glad. True religion always begins with our emotions. The tragedy comes when we let it end there.

In my own church, a frail little woman came to her pastor saying she would like a place of service. Her heart had been stirred and she wanted to render service. He gave her a class of boys to teach. That was thirty-five years ago, but she has continued to teach that same class. Later on some girls were added to the class. Of course, they are grown men and women now. But through all those many years Miss Emma Wilson has been with them. There have been Sundays when the weather was bad, or when she wanted to go somewhere else, or when she had a headache, but except for the few times when she was out of the city or sick in bed, she has been in her place of service.

Once a man got so enthusiastic he said to Jesus, "Lord, I will follow thee whithersoever thou goest." But Jesus could see he was only gushing with emotional feeling and was not prepared to pay the price. So the Lord said, "Foxes have holes, and birds of the air have nests; but the Son of man hath not where to lay his head" (Luke 9:57-58). The Lord was telling the man that there is sacrifice involved.

Every church roll contains the names of a number of people who join without realizing that it takes time, patience and effort really to become a member of the church. They are not willing to work their way in and are disappointed when all the church program does not revolve around them. A man said to me recently, "I will join your church if you will give me a place of service." I said, "You can join the church but you must win your place."

After that great experience on the Mount of Transfiguration, Peter wanted to stay up there. But Christ knew that down below was an opportunity of service. Many want the experience, but fall out when the service begins. It is as the minister said to a late-comer who asked, "Is the service over?" He replied, "The worship is over but the service has just begun." That is as it should be.

AMONG THORNS

(3) Some seed fell "among thorns." There are a lot of fine and capable people represented here. They receive the word of God, and they earnestly desire to serve God. But then they take on so many other interests that gradually God is choked out. We hear a lot about the possibility of being destroyed by atomic bombs. I think the greatest danger in America is that we will be "clubbed" to death. There are a lot of people running themselves sick trying to get to all their club meetings.

In the spring of the year a farmer will thin out his cotton. He knows his land will produce a better yield with fewer stalks. We need to thin out our activities and give ourselves time to concentrate on the ones that really matter. Someone has well said, "Many people give first-rate loyalties to second-rate causes." The three most important institutions are the church, the home, and the school.

There is still something more important to say. One of the mightiest of the knights of old was Sir Lancelot, but he failed in his quest for the Holy Grail. He honestly tells us why he failed:

. . . but in me lived a sin
So strange, of such a kind, that all of pure
Noble and knightly in me twined and clung
Round that one sin, until the poisonous grew
Together, each as each,
Not to be plucked asunder.

The Word of God can grow in your heart. Also, a sin, even a little sin, grows. And they both cannot grow together. If we do not want God enough to give up that wrong, eventually the garden of our souls will be overrun with the wrong. It works this way: First it is your sin, but little by little your sin becomes you.

We have a way of doing what we know is wrong, but we excuse ourselves by saying, "It won't count this time." In answer to that, the great psychologist William James said: "You may not count it but it is being counted, just the same. Down among your nerve cells and fibers the molecules are counting it, registering, storing it up to be used against you when the next temptation comes." Yes, your sin will eventually become you.

GOOD GROUND

Finally, some seed falls on "good ground." I can't explain the miracle of the seed, neither can any other person. I hold in my hand a tiny grain of corn. I throw it into the ground. Soon the life in that seed bursts forth and a green shoot appears. Gradually the stalk grows and at the proper time the ear of corn develops. Then comes the harvest and our prayer—"Give us this day our daily bread"—is answered.

Far more wonderful is how the Word of God takes lodgment in our hearts. It grows and gradually takes possession of our desires, our emotions, our thoughts, and of our actions. And little by little our lives become happy, fruitful and like God. Some people are "good ground."

11. MAINTAIN YOUR FORGIVENESS

The Parable of the Unmerciful Servant

MATTHEW 18:21-35

A VERY THOUGHT-PROVOKING AND DISTURBING QUESTION
was asked me: "If God fully forgives a person, is there
a possibility of Him ever taking back that forgiveness?"
My first impulse is to say "No. Once God forgives any
wrong that is the end of it forever." Children sometimes
call each other "Indian-givers." That means to give something to the other but later take it back. That indicates
changeableness that you expect in children but certainly
not in God.

A criminal can be tried and convicted of some
crime. Later the governor of the state may pardon that
man. If so, never again can the criminal be tried for
that offense. He might be tried for other crimes, but a
crime once pardoned is forever settled. We think of
forgiveness as pardon, and we have always felt that
God's forgiveness was irrevocable.

However, if we study closely a story Jesus told, we
might see the forgiveness of God in a different light. He
told about a servant who owed his king ten thousand
talents. That was an enormous amount of money, about

two million dollars. It was impossible for him to pay it. So, when the king had the servant brought before him, the man pleaded his inability and the king forgave him the debt.

The servant went his way but soon met one of his fellow servants who owed him a hundred pence, only about twenty dollars. He demanded payment of the debt, but the servant did not have it. Though he pleaded, he was thrown into jail. His pleas fell on deaf ears, he received no mercy. It is hard to believe that a man who had just been forgiven such a large debt, would refuse to extend mercy to another. Though he had received so much forgiveness, he refused to pass on even a little forgiveness.

The king heard about it and had the man called back before him, reminding the servant, "I forgave thee all that debt." But because he refused to show the right spirit toward his fellow servant, the king had him thrown in jail "till he should pay all that was due unto him." The king's forgiveness was cancelled and the debt was restored. And Jesus adds: "So likewise shall my heavenly Father do also unto you, if ye from your hearts forgive not every one his brother their trespasses."

To attain God's forgiveness requires, first, a recognition of our debt. That is conviction. The servant did not argue about what he owed, he did not try to excuse himself. Second, though he cannot pay the debt, still he means to do his best from then on. He will make what restitution he can, and certainly he does not intend to go further in debt. That is repentance and change. The king shows mercy. Justice would have forever doomed the man. It was only mercy that brought about his forgiveness. Conviction—repentance—mercy, those three added together bring forgiveness.

But this story warns us that God's forgiveness of us and our forgiveness of others are forever linked together. Have you ever done wrong? If so, you stand in need of God's forgiveness. Has any person ever done you wrong? If so, what have you done about it?

WE, TOO, MUST FORGIVE

Peter asked Jesus, "Lord, how oft shall my brother sin against me, and I forgive him? till seven times?" Seven times is a lot of times. Some of us have not been able to forgive even one time. But Jesus replied, "Until seventy times seven" (Matt. 18:21-35). By that He does not mean four hundred and ninety times but rather does He mean that forgiveness must be a continuing experience.

Just as the water flows continually from the spring, so must forgiveness flow from our hearts. Jesus told the story of the king who cancelled his forgiveness of the servant who owed him ten thousand talents because that servant refused to show the same spirit toward one of his fellows who owed him. Thereby Jesus warns us that when we stop our forgiveness of others, God stops His forgiveness of us.

Forgiveness is much more than just not holding something against another. It further means restoration, helping the person to be his best. I think of three people it is very difficult for us to have the attitude of forgiveness toward.

(1) There is the person who does not belong to our group. Once the Apostle John saw a man casting out devils. He was doing a good work, but John says, "We forbade him, because he followeth not with us" (Mark 9:38).

Deep in our hearts we admit that all the churches are working to save sinners and for the glory of God. Yet, it is hard to feel happy over the success of some church or minister who does not belong to our group. We know that God made all the different races of the earth, and we know that every man regardless of color or creed, is a child of God. Yet, it is so easy to feel prejudice. We know that some people have attained more material and social success than others, and it is difficult to keep from getting a little snobbish.

Gladstone once wrote his wife that he has "no opportunity of pardoning others, for none offend me." But even so, there is the positive side of forgiveness which sends us out from our comfort and complacency, as it did the shepherd, to find some sheep who was not in the fold.

(2) Another person we find it hard to forgive is the one who does us wrong. The one who refuses to give us the attention and consideration we think we deserve. I know a man today who is past fifty years old, yet his heart is filled with bitterness because he failed to receive a bid to a college fraternity. Maybe you have been slighted, maybe somebody has spoken evil of you, maybe somebody has done you some other wrong. To not hold resentment takes a lot. To go further and really in your heart wish that person good, is even harder to do.

(3) The hardest person to forgive is the one you have wronged. Who do you love the most—the person who does the most for you or the person for whom you do the most? As you are walking down the street, which person had you rather meet—the person who has done you a favor or the person you have done something for? Which loves the most—a mother or a child? The beginning of love is service.

Likewise, it is far easier to forgive someone who has wronged you than someone you have wronged. When another has done the wrong, it is his duty, whether he does it or not, to get on his knees. But when you have done the wrong, it is your place to get on your knees, and that is hard to do.

Remember forgiveness of others is the price God charges for His forgiveness of us.

TO HELP YOU FORGIVE

Jesus taught us to pray, "Forgive us our sins, as we forgive those who sin against us." He further said, "If ye forgive men their trespasses, your heavenly Father will also forgive you" (Matt. 6:12-14). That is both a glorious promise and an awful warning. To forgive every person, excepting none, is just about the hardest thing we are called on to do. Yet unless we forgive, we cannot be forgiven.

The main reason most of us do not forgive is simply because we do not want to. Before you realize it, bitterness against some other person will spread over your system like a fast growing cancer. It will make you sour and irritable. You develop a martyr-complex, and you begin to pity yourself. Before long you even begin to enjoy your misery. And gradually you become the most hopeless creature on earth. To cure a body afflicted with, for example, cancer, is far easier than to take out of one's soul an unforgiving spirit.

I have two suggestions that will succeed whenever they are sincerely tried. (1) Take a sheet of paper and across the top write "The Sins Of My Life." Sit down quietly and write down everything you can remember that you have done wrong. Forget about that other person until you finish making your own list. When you have written down all the wrongs and faults of your life you can remember, put the paper aside but keep thinking and as additional things come to mind, add them to the list.

It will be a painful experience. In fact, it will give you a taste of what hell is like. Speaking of hell, Paterson Smyth wrote:

And the ghosts of forgotten actions
Came floating before my sight,
And the things that I thought were dead things,
Were alive with a terrible might.

And the vision of all my past life,
Was an awful thing to face
Alone, alone with my conscience,
In that strange and terrible place.

When you finish your list, then take another sheet of paper and put down whatever it is you do not want to or feel you cannot forgive in that other person.

Then compare the two lists. You will see immediately the point in the story Jesus told of the man who was forgiven a debt of two million dollars yet refused to forgive another of only twenty dollars. You will be so ashamed and you will feel so acutely your own need that you will fall on your knees praying, "God be merciful to me a sinner."

But then you will hear our Lord saying, "But if ye forgive not men their trespasses, neither will your Father forgive you" (Matt. 6:15). And as you think of your own need of God's forgiveness, you will find it easy to forgive every person you hold anything against. Lord Herbert once said, "He who will not forgive another has broken the bridge over which he himself must pass."

(2) My second suggestion for those who find it hard to forgive is, after you have looked carefully at your own sins, lift your eyes away from yourself and "that other person" and look at Christ. Watch the soldiers take Him that night in Gethsemane, follow Him through His humiliating trials, feel the lash as it is laid on His back, walk with Him up Calvary, watch the nails as they are driven through His flesh, note His embarrassment as He is stripped bare before that uncouth mob.

You will want to turn away but don't miss seeing them spit on Him and ridicule and laugh as He is dying. And then listen as He says, "Father, forgive them." With the picture of your sins and of Him on the cross, forgiveness of others will come within easy reach for you.

12. BE READY FOR YOUR OPPORTUNITY

The Parable of the Ten Bridesmaids

MATTHEW 25:1-13

ONE OF THE BEST KNOWN STORIES OF ALL TIME IS THE one about the ten bridesmaids. In Jesus' day the groom with his groomsmen would go to the bride's house where she and her bridesmaids would be waiting, and the entire party would have a grand processional through the streets back to his house for a great marriage ceremony.

They had no street lights in that day and one of the chief functions of the bridesmaids was to carry lamps to light the way. On this particular night the ten maids all had their lamps and were at the bride's house ready and waiting. Expecting the groom at any moment, their lamps were lighted. However, the groom was late in coming and all the maids went to sleep. It was midnight before the cry finally went up, "Behold, the bridegroom cometh; go ye out to meet him."

Immediately they arose and trimmed their lamps. But because of the long delay, the oil in their lamps was burned up. However, five of the girls had thought to bring an additional vessel of oil and quickly they could refill their lamps. The other five had not foreseen the long delay and thus had brought no reserve supply.

In consternation they begged for the loan of some oil. But those who had an extra supply turned them down and said, "Not so; lest there be not enough for us and you: but go ye rather to them that sell, and buy for yourselves." The five went to buy, but at the hour of midnight it was difficult to find a shop open and when finally they did get some oil and got back, they found that the procession was over, the bridal party was in the house and the door was locked. They begged to get in but the doorkeeper refused them, and they were left out in the dark.

That is a very simple story, easy to picture in our minds and understand, yet it illustrates the profoundest fact of success in life:—namely, the attainment of heaven. Of course, this story may refer to the attainment of heaven in the hereafter, but it also illustrates the attainment of heaven in the here and now. For most of us heaven means a place which God has prepared where we live in perfect happiness and peace.

It doesn't necessarily follow that the only heaven you can experience is the one you will go to after you die. If heaven means a life lived in harmony with God and according to His plan and purpose for each of us, and it does mean that, then you do not have to die to experience it. You can have the kingdom of heaven now, in a much more limited degree, but just the same it will be heaven.

We read, "In my Father's house are many mansions . . . I go to prepare a place for you" (John 14:2). We

also read, "The earth is the Lord's, and the fulness
thereof; the world and they that dwell therein" (Psalm
24:1). So we are living in one of God's houses right
now and right here and now we can taste heaven.

A GREAT MOMENT OF DESTINY FOR YOU

Jesus told the story of the ten bridesmaids to illustrate the coming of heaven for each person. Some say
this story refers to the time of our death. That we know
not when it will happen and therefore we must be ready.
Others feel it refers to the second coming of Christ.
But I rather think Jesus means that for each and every
person God has prepared a great hour of opportunity
—a moment of destiny. Shakespeare said it well:—

> There is a tide in the affairs of men,
> Which, taken at the flood, leads on to fortune;
> Omitted, all the voyage of their life,
> Is bound in shallows and in miseries.
> On such a full sea are we now afloat;
> And we must take the current when it serves,
> Or lose our ventures.

Certainly Jesus believed in the one moment of
destiny for Himself. As a boy of twelve He is conscious
of the fact that God had a purpose for His life (Luke
2:49). Yet it must have seemed a long wait for Him,
a very long wait. For eighteen years and longer He
waited. During that time He worked in a carpenter's
shop. It must have been boresome, lowly work for Him.
Yet, He did the job before him.

But along with His daily work, He grew. The
Bible says He grew "in wisdom and stature, and in favor

with God and man (Luke 2:52). Before God could bring His hour, there must be preparation for it. He developed His mind, He took care of His body, He became better and better acquainted with God, He learned to love other people. But still He waited. Early in His ministry He said to His mother, "Mine hour is not yet come" (John 2:4). But one day He says, "For this cause came I unto this hour," and He was ready.

Now that same Christ says to me and to you, "As my Father hath sent me, even so send I you" (John 20:21). He reminded us of the shepherd who thought of his sheep not as a flock, but as one by one. So, when one was missing, out into the darkness the shepherd goes to find it. God counts us not as people but as persons. He made you and you and you for a purpose. And one day He will put His hand on your shoulder and say "Now." If you are prepared, you can walk with Him into the kingdom of heaven. For those not prepared, the door was shut and they were left in the darkness. Someone has pointed out there are three things you can never recall—the sped arrow, the spoken word, and the lost opportunity.

But is there no second opportunity? In the story Jesus told of the wise and foolish bridesmaids there wasn't. Maybe there were other weddings, and maybe they learned their lesson. But this chance was gone forever. Maybe God is holding back your one hour of opportunity, your moment of destiny, until you are ready. That would be a merciful thing for Him to do, and we are taught He is a God of mercy. If that be true, maybe He is at this moment ready, if you are ready.

There are some who are bitter and unhappy, frus-

trated and disappointed. They see no meaning and purpose in life, they have lost heart. Well, who can those
people blame? Not God. He had an opportunity for each
one and that opportunity is your doorway into heaven.

GOD HAS ALL ETERNITY

I have been talking about Jesus' story of the ten
bridesmaids and saying that for every person God has
prepared an hour of opportunity—a moment of destiny.
I believe there are many who have missed God's call
because they were expecting something spectacular. God
made most of us for very ordinary places.

Someone has figured out that since the beginning
of recorded history about thirty billion people have
been born. Out of that number historians would say
only about 5,000 have done outstanding things. That
means there is only one in every 6,000,000. But that
does not matter. What does matter is whether or not
we are happy. Heaven means being happy, and Jesus
says when we hear and accept God's call, then heaven
has come for us. That is what we want, both in this life
and in the next. When a person has heaven, nothing
else really matters.

Much of my ministry has been spent talking with
people for whom it seems the door has never opened.
Things happen I cannot explain—a wife and children
with a drunken husband and father, one born with a
deformed body, a lovely lady with a deep instinct for a
home and children never getting the chance for them,
the young man who had to quit school to support a
sick parent, and many others.

Time and again I have had to say, "I do not know what God will open for you but because I believe so strongly in Him and His purposes, I believe that all of your suffering, endurance, patience and faithfulness will somehow become a part of your heaven when finally He puts His hand on your shoulder and says 'Now.' "

But some say to me, "Now I am old, now it is too late." My answer to that is, while we think in terms of the short span of one life, God has all eternity. Whether you now realize it or not, you have all of eternity, too. Take from me that assurance and I would be unable to make any sense of this universe and life as we find it.

"Ah, but a man's reach should exceed his grasp, Or what is heaven for?" said Browning.

One further thought—though God gives us our hour of opportunity, the preparation for it He leaves in our hands. The only way to prepare for tomorrow is to face honestly and bravely the living of each day as we come to it. As we take Christ as our Saviour and our daily companion, we begin storing up oil in our lamps for the opportunity coming. Someone wrote these words:

> Very dear the Cross of Shame
> Where He took the sinner's blame,
> And the tomb wherein He lay
> Until the third day came.
>
> But He walked the self-same road
> And He bore the self-same load,
> When the Carpenter of Nazareth
> Made common things for God.

The wise virgins seem cruel in refusing to share their oil, but that is the way it must be. Courage, faith, character in the hour of opportunity cannot be obtained from someone else. But each time I express faith, I am storing it up to be used again. Each time I face life triumphantly, though it be in a very small and obscure matter, I am preparing for my great moment. May I begin that preparation now.

13. FINDING THE JOY OF THE LORD

The Parable of the Talents
MATTHEW 25:14-30

ONCE A MAN WAS PREPARING TO TAKE A LONG JOURNEY, but before he left he turned his money over to three trusted employees and told them to manage it for him. To one man he gave five talents, to another two, and to another one. The first two men used the money in trades and doubled what they had received. But the third man was afraid to do anything with his, so he buried it in the ground. When the master returned home, he was pleased with the two who used the money but very harsh with the third man. Jesus told that story to illustrate our responsibility to God.

From that story we learn some important truths. For instance, we see that men are not equally endowed. Some people have more brains and abilities than others. Some are born with a stronger and more attractive physical body than others, some are given better opportunities. I once heard a man say, "I can do anything anybody else can do." That statement is simply not true. No person can do everything.

One point of the story is that in every person God

has invested some ability, and it is not my business to compare myself with others, but rather to use what I have in the best way I can. When I listen to some great preacher, I realize I can't preach like he can. I wish I could but I know I can't. So there comes the feeling that I ought not to try to preach. Then I realize that he can't preach like I can. I believe God made me. I sometimes wonder why He would make anybody like me but since He did, it is my business to do the best I can and not be envious of any other person.

God made you. Into you He put some talents and He expects you to use them. In his lovely poem, "The Day And The Work," Edwin Markham tells us:

> There is waiting a work where only your
>   hands can avail;
> And so if you falter, a chord in the music will
>   fail.

It lifts every person to a thrilling sense of importance to realize that the eternal God needed you and so He made you.

WHAT A TALENT IS

From this story comes our word "talent." Originally it meant money and it still means that. Certainly how we use our money is important. But it means much more. If people can do things like sing, or sew beautifully, or make a speech, we say they are talented. God holds us accountable for those special abilities. There are, however, still greater talents.

There is a song, "I sing because I'm happy." But

some people have learned to sing yet never learned to be happy. If there had to be a choice. I had rather live with someone who has the talent for being cheerful than singing. Sympathy, serenity, loyalty, kindness—there are many talents. And to each one is given some talent.

To those who used their talents, the master said, "Well done, thou good and faithful servant." Notice, he did not say "successful" servant. Faithfulness is ours to give. Success is God's to give. No man is condemned because he is not equal in ability to some other, no man is condemned who tries and fails, but to the man who refused to try, the master said, "Cast ye the unprofitable servant into outer darkness."

WHY HE WAS AFRAID

In Jesus' story of the talents, one man utterly failed. He was not a bad fellow. He neither stole his master's money nor wasted it in riotous living. He simply buried it and did nothing. In explanation he says, "I was afraid." There are a lot of people like him. They are not doing much wrong, but neither are they doing much good. They are paralyzed by fear. As you read the story, you find several things of which he might have been afraid.

First, because he only had one talent while others had five and two, he was afraid he could not make as big a showing as they could. He knew he could not be the most outstanding, so he would not be anything. No doubt he sat back and told himself and others what wonderful things he would do, if only he had ten talents.

I can speak here from experience. For example, more than once have I dreamed of the wonderful things

I would do if I had had John D. Rockefeller's wealth. I would have built schools, hospitals, churches, helped the poor. I would have been so good and generous. When I dream about that, I feel mighty proud of myself. Then one day I learned a little poem that disturbs me. It says:

> It's not what you'd do with a million
> If riches should be your lot;
> But what are you doing today
> With the dollar and a quarter you've got?

Rockefeller did have millions, but there was a time when he made only $4.50 a week and he gave a tithe of that.

A lot of people are afraid of their littleness. If they can't be the soloist in the choir, they sit back in sour silence and refuse to sing at all. Back of this fear is a false and silly pride.

Second, he was afraid of the possibility of failure. He says to his master, "I knew thee that thou art a hard man," and if he failed he felt he would be severely condemned. People are sometimes cruel in their judgments, but I notice that most people will go out of the way to help one who sincerely tries. When it comes to the judgment of God, we need have no fear. He knows all the circumstances. God expects us to have faith in Him and in ourselves. The victories are won by those who believe they can.

Third, this one-talent man was afraid of work. He was called a "slothful" servant. A lot of us like to sing the old Negro spiritual, "I want to go to heaven, sitting down." Read the lives of great people and you find they all had one thing in common—they worked hard. False pride, lack of faith, laziness can so paralyze your life that you wither away into nothing.

Talents are like seed. Plant the seed and they multiply. Lay them on the shelf and eventually the life goes out of them. "Take the talent from him," said the master. That is simply one of the unbreakable laws of life. You can take fresh strawberries, put them into your freezer and months later they will still have their freshness.

Not so with yourself. Bury your talents and the law of life says, "Take the talent from him." The only way to preserve yourself is to live.

WORK WELL DONE

"Enter thou into the joy of thy lord." That is one of the most thrilling and beautiful statements in the Bible. That is what we all want. Why do we seek certain things—recognition, possession, health, security, friends, peace of mind? It is because we feel those things will bring us joy. The basic desire of all of us is to be happy. In His story of the talents, Jesus tells us that to each is given some ability and opportunity. Ours may be much less than what is given to some other. But when one accepts himself as he is, and uses what he has as best he can, there comes to him "the joy of his lord." Notice in the story, one man had five talents and another two, but each received the same joy. I may not be able to accomplish as much as some others, but, I can be just as happy as any man can be.

I remember so well the Sunday I began my ministry.

I preached that morning on the Prodigal Son and I tried to say I believed in a Father who would welcome back home his wandering boy. Since then I have preached that sermon many times. That Sunday night I preached on: "How To Sleep Well On A Windy Night." I have never preached that sermon again. Maybe it was not worth repeating, but I did have one story in it that is good.

A boy went to a farmer and asked to be given a job as a hired hand. The farmer asked, "Are you willing to work?" "Please sir, yes sir, I can sleep well on a windy night," was his strange reply. "Can I trust you to look after my things?", the farmer asked. Again he replied, "Please sir, yes sir, I can sleep well on a windy night." The farmer asked several questions seeking to determine if the boy were honest and trustworthy, but to each question he got only that one reply.

He decided the boy might be a little foolish, but there was something about him the farmer liked. So he hired him. The boy proved to be a willing worker and everything went well until one night a big storm came up. The farmer heard it and rushed up to the boy's room. "Get up," he shouted, "let's go tie down the hay stacks, put up the tools and secure the barn doors." But the boy was so sound asleep the farmer could not wake him. Fearing to waste time trying to get him up, he rushed out to see about the things.

When he came to the haystacks, he found them already firmly tied. He found the tools in their proper places in the barn and the doors closed securely. As he went back into the house he realized what the boy had meant about sleeping well on a windy night. He meant that each day he did his job as best as he could and, even in the midst of a storm, he could sleep.

The Bible tells us, the Lord "giveth his beloved sleep" (Psalm 127:2). When one recognizes the fact that God made him for a purpose and that to him God gave some abilities, and when one consecrates himself to God and seeks to do his best, there does come to him a restful peace. It is indeed "the joy of thy Lord."

14. THE MAN GOD CALLED A FOOL

The Parable of the Rich Farmer
LUKE 12:13-21

I HAVE ALWAYS FELT THERE WAS SOMETHING MORE IN Jesus' story of the rich farmer than I have been able to dig out. It contains all the elements to make a great story. There is work and success, there is wealth and laughter, friends and security, wisdom and foolishness, romance and adventure and it all ends in tragedy. But let's begin at the beginning.

It is about a man who was a farmer. Farming is probably the most ancient and satisfying profession one can follow. Adam and Eve were farmers. In their garden they grew their food and clothes, and through all the centuries we have recognized our dependence on the farmer. I know of people who claim to have no need of a pastor, or a physician, or a banker. But I have never known one to declare his independence of the farmer. If the farmers all quit work for one year, all the world would starve to death.

There is romance in farming. The farmer plows the ground and buries his seed with faith that life in the seed will burst forth, that the seasons will come and he will gather the harvest. On the farm you are close to nature. Nothing is grander than such things as the feel of new plowed soil, the blossoms of the apple trees, the call of the bobwhite, the fragrance of new-mown hay, the clean air about you. Someone has said that the typical American success story is the boy who grows up on a farm, moves to the city, works hard and makes money, buys a farm and moves back to live on it.

This man was rich. His ground "brought forth plentifully." So much so that he had no place to store all he produced. I have heard of people who had so much money they did not know what to do with it. I don't know any people like that. I wish I did. I would cultivate their friendship and do my best to help them solve that particular problem.

I know of a preacher who once preached on "What I Would Do With A Million Dollars." After the service a man came up and handed him a check for that amount. I wish that same man would come to hear me preach. I am not mad at rich people. I like to have them around.

This farmer was interested in saving what he made. That is not wrong. God saves. When God created the earth, He put a lot of water on it and through all the centuries He has kept every drop of it. Not one grain of the earth's sand has ever been lost. After Jesus fed the multitude, He had the disciples gather up the fragments that none be wasted.

To be a successful farmer requires hard work, so we know this man was not lazy. There is no hint of dishonesty in the story. We must assume that he paid his workers a fair wage, that he sold his goods at the right price. He was not excessively greedy. He did not try to buy up all the land in the country. In fact, when he found he had enough for his needs, he was willing to stand back and let others have an opportunity.

There is an old Moslem teaching to the effect that craving wealth is like drinking sea water. The more you drink the more your thirst increases, and you keep on drinking until you perish. But this farmer knew when he had enough. Still, God called him a fool.

WHY HE WAS A FOOL

For the answer turn back to Psalm 14. There we read, "The fool hath said in his heart, there is no God." If you asked that rich farmer, "Do you believe there is a God?" He doubtless would have said, "Certainly I do." He could have given many reasons why he so believed, but all of his reasons would have been from his mind.

When it came to his feelings, his heart, he had left God out. Why? Because he did not feel the need of God. There is a vast difference between believing in your mind and believing in your heart. For example, I have had people talk to me about Divine healing and say they believed there is something to it. On the other hand, in the middle of the night I have gone to the hospital to pray with a father and mother whose baby was about to die. Their belief is vastly different because they feel the need so deeply.

We can talk about the forgiveness of sin and say we believe in it. But let some person sit in the pastor's study or kneel at the altar whose soul is darkened by a deep sense of guilt. They have tried forgetting it, thinking of something else, moral reform, but nothing has worked.

The peace and laughter have gone out of their lives, and in its place dwells remorse and fear. As that person looks up to God, it is not mere intellectual belief, it comes from the heart.

The possession of wealth is not wrong. Jesus never said it was. But it is the most dangerous thing in life. Jesus talked about money more than any other subject. Remember this: He was talking to poor people. Many times we hear someone say, "I don't want to be rich. All I want is just enough to live on comfortably and to take care of me when I get old." That is all the farmer in Jesus' story wanted, but God called him a fool.

Jesus said at the conclusion of this story, "So is he that layeth up treasure for himself, and is not rich toward God." This man thought about himself. He talks about "My fruits," "My goods," "My barns." He says, "I shall do this," "I shall do that." My—My—My—I—I—I.

Instead of gratitude, his success brought pride. Instead of a sense of obligation to his fellowman, he thinks only of his own pleasure and needs. Instead of faith in God, he put his confidence in things.

The man reached the point that he felt no need of God. He was sufficient unto himself. Jesus said such a person is a fool. It worries me to hear someone say, "It is my duty to go to church." I don't want anybody coming to my church from a sense of duty. I want people to come from a sense of need. It is not necessary to talk to a thirsty man about the body's need of water. You only have to put the water before him.

When a person thinks about things, measures suc-

a fellowship with Him who owns the land on both sides of the river. This was the wealth that one man swapped for barns. God did not say he was bad. He said he was a fool.

15. REMEMBER WHO YOU ARE

The Parable of the Unjust Steward
LUKE 16:1-9

JESUS HAD MORE TO SAY ABOUT MONEY THAN ANY OTHER subject. He began His preaching by saying, "Repent ye," and throughout His ministry He emphasized the necessity of repentance. Yet He talked about money more than He did repentance. He talked to people about forgiveness, about happiness, about eternal life. He emphasized the power of faith and the strength of love. Yet He talked more about money than any of these things. One third of all His parables and one sixth of all the verses in the four Gospels are about money.

Why did He talk so much about money? Certainly He did not try to get money for Himself. I do not recall a single instance of Him taking a collection. As far as we know His only possession was the cloak which He wore. He wanted to capture the souls of men for God, and He knew that money was His chief rival. "You cannot serve God and mammon," He said (Luke 16:13).

He wanted people to serve God with the same intelligence and enthusiasm with which they served money. People will get up early every morning, hurry to a job and work all day in order to get money. Some people will take all the money they have and use it to build a factory or a store or some other business in order to get more money. Some people will steal, lie, even murder, to get money. Never one time did Jesus condemn money. He never said it was wrong to earn money.

The trouble with money is it can make us so shortsighted. We can forget there is anything else to life, and we can make the ministering to our physical needs and desires the main goal of our lives. Therein lies the danger of money. And when money becomes our God, we always end up disappointed. Judas let money blind him to the things of life that really counted. He got money and then realized what a sorry bargain he had made. He cast his money away and went out and hanged himself. The one who gives his life to material things eventually discovers that neither the things nor the life are worth having.

There was the rich farmer who became so satisfied with his material possessions. "But God said unto him, Thou fool, this night thy soul shall be required of thee: then whose shall those things be, which thou has provided?" (Luke 12.20). That man never saw beyond his money. He never thought ahead.

Jesus talked about stewardship. That does not mean we are not to possess material things. In fact, you must possess something in order to be a steward. But stewardship means looking beyond to the higher uses of money.

FRIENDS ARE MORE IMPORTANT

Suppose you were to take an inventory of all your material possessions. It would include your money in the bank, your bonds, your car, house, jewelry and everything. Now suppose God told you that exactly a month from today He would take all that you have away from you, but until that time you could use it exactly as you pleased. What would you do? Would you get panicky and do nothing? Would you rush out and give it all away? Would you have one last big fling? What would you do?

Jesus told us a story of a man in just such a situation. (Luke 16:1-9). This man had been looking after the wealth of another man, but his employer became dissatisfied with him and called for an accounting in order to close him out. To begin with, the man said to himself, "What shall I do?" I like that. He was face to face with calamity. He was losing his job, his position in the community, the security he had enjoyed and all that he had.

He realized that the calamity had fallen upon him, and there was now nothing he could do about that. There is no need to waste time in foolish regrets and in wishing he had done differently. Even though his calamity was brought on by his own mistakes, it was too late to change them. So very wisely he began to work out some plan of action. This man said, "I am resolved what to do." That is the first step to victory.

So often people let some set-back take all the heart out of them. Some piously fold their hands and say it is the Lord's will. Some become bitter and resentful. "I don't know what I have done to deserve this. God is not fair." Some go about telling their troubles to all who will listen, seeking sympathy and a shoulder to cry on. When Leland Stanford lost his only son he said, "I will build a university to help other boys." For those who will work for it, every tragedy can bring a triumph. If we keep looking, we will eventually see the silver lining in every cloud.

The prospect of losing his money made this man realize his dependence on other people. He realizes he is too old to get out and dig, he was ashamed to beg. So he decided that he would go out and help as many people as he could; thus, when he was down and out, they would help him. His motives were utterly selfish but even so, he learned a great lesson. One of the chief dangers of possessions is we develop a false sense of independence. One of the greatest mistakes a man can make is to swap a friend for some material gain.

So he stopped thinking about getting and started thinking about giving. I am sure that before long something wonderful began happening to him. He began to feel the warmth of friendship, to receive the smiles of appreciation, to have the inner satisfaction of realizing that his life counts for something. Without doubt he began to realize how much better stewardship is than possessing. Someone said there are three kicks in money. One comes in making it, another comes in having it. The third comes in giving it. Those who miss the third kick miss the best one of the three.

THE ECONOMIC LAWS OF GOD

Jesus illustrates the economic laws of God with this story of the rich man who permitted a servant to be the steward of a portion of his wealth. However, one day the master called the steward in and announced that soon his stewardship would end. As the man thought over his situation, three definite facts became clear to him.

(1) The wealth he had been using was not his own. That is a principle a lot of people overlook. Everything we have was put here in the creation by God. He retained title to it but allows us to use what we can possess. But possession does not mean ownership. There is the story of the little boy who was given two nickels—one for Sunday school and the other for himself. As he was running down the street he dropped one of them and watched it roll into the sewer. "Well," he muttered, "there goes God's nickel." But the truth is all the nickels are God's.

(2) Though he had complete possession of the wealth, could do with it as he pleased, his possession was temporary. Just a little while ago someone else possessed it, and in a short time it will pass on into other hands. These possessions we have will be here as long as the world exists, but we won't be here.

(3) How I use my possessions now, determines my wealth tomorrow. There are people who think that tithing is merely a scheme to raise money. Such is not the case. Tithing is God's plan for the financing of the work of His kingdom. It is also His program to develop within people a sense of partnership with God. Tithing does something for your soul. The tragedy of material things is that it has the power to make man forget he has a soul.

One of the highlights of the career of Roland Hayes was when he was invited to sing before the king in Buckingham Palace. His parents had been slaves, and he was born in a tiny cabin in Georgia. His father died when Roland was a boy, but he was brought up by a good mother who taught him the important principles of living. A music teacher heard him sing and doors for him began to open. Amazing opportunities all over the world became his. Finally the door of Buckingham Palace opened to him.

He was delighted and sent his mother a cablegram telling her about it. She cabled back to him a message of just four words: "Remember who you are." That was just what he needed. It is just what I need—what you need. It is so easy to forget ourselves, to get carried away with the things of this world. As we face the daily grind to make a living, it is easy to forget there is more to us than just our bodies.

We must remember who we are. The Bible tells us how God made man out of the dust of the earth. We are also told that our bodies will go back to dust. The Bible also tells us that God breathed into man "the breath of life; and man became a living soul." Don't let your dust make you forget your soul. Remember who you are.

16. FOUNDATION FOR A LIFE

The Parable of the Two Builders
MATTHEW 7:24-27

HAVE YOU EVER WRITTEN A SERMON? IT IS A VERY INTER-
esting experience. Every sermon ought to begin in prayer
because the minister who does not talk with God in his
study, cannot talk for God in his pulpit. Through prayer
one begins to feel the spirit of God and to understand
the mind of God. Also, the minister must have in mind
the people who are going to hear his sermon. He must
love them and want his sermon to help them. A sermon
that doesn't help the hearer is not worth preaching.

With God and the people in his heart, the preacher
is then ready to begin preparing his sermon. First, he
needs a good foundation. Shakespeare said: "there are
sermons in stones." But the best sermons are based on
some passage of the Bible, which is the revealed truth
of God. The purpose of the sermon is to make clear
God's truth and then inspire the hearer to do something
about it.

Jesus said, "Whosoever heareth these sayings of
mine, and doeth them." That is a good foundation text
on which to build a sermon. Immediately you see that

the two key words are "heareth" and "doeth." What
was it He wanted the people to hear? To answer that
you must go back and read what He had just said. It is
recorded in Matthew five, six, and seven.

He had just finished telling the people that happiness is based not on possession but on character. Meekness, a hunger and thirst for righteousness, and purity of
heart are some of the qualities of character He men-
tioned. He speaks of the importance of the law, but He
says to fulfill the law one must develop the right spirit
in his heart. For example, to fulfill the law against murder, put love in your heart and let it drive out your hate,
your jealousy, and your feeling of being treated
wrongly.

He says to help your fellowmen because you love
them rather than to build up your own reputation. He
says we ought to learn to pray and to put our trust in
God. He speaks of deciding which master we will serve
and He makes clear the fact that, if one puts God first,
the other things we really want in life just naturally
come.

But it is not enough just to hear the truth. The hearing ought to do three things for us. First, it should stir
our feelings. Some people say we should leave emotion
out of our religion, but a person without feelings is a
dead person. When you see one of God's truths it should
stir your heart. Second, the hearing should stimulate
your thinking. The Bible says, "Come now, and let us
reason together" (Isaiah 1:18). Without reins on the
horse, he would run wild. And without reason and in-
telligent thinking, our emotions get out of hand.

But it is not enough for a sermon just to make us feel good or to make us think. Jesus used the word "doeth." The sermon should inspire us to some action. Discussions of religion may be enjoyable, but we need to remember that Jesus said, "He that doeth the will of my Father." So every sermon should begin with a truth and end in a life.

ROCK OR SAND

One of the amazing things about the preaching of Jesus was how He could make so clear the eternal truths of God with such ordinary illustrations. For example, He shows that building your life is like building a house. We can build either on the rock or on the sand. The sand He was referring to was the wide, dry river beds there in Palestine.

These beds were made by the melting snow coming down from the mountains. Maybe only once in a generation would the snows be so heavy as to be dangerous when they melted. Most of the time there was a nice little stream trickling down through the bottom of the wide bed. There on the sand it was an easy place to build and convenient to live. The sand was nice, the water was near and in the winter it was a sheltered place from the cold winds.

On the other hand, to build up on the rocks was difficult. It meant grading the side of the hill and it was burdensome to carry up the materials. After the house was built, living up there was harder. The water had to be "toted," the poor fuel they had to burn was not sufficient to overcome the cold of the winter. So, it was a great temptation to build down on the sand.

So it is with building a life on the principles which Jesus taught. It isn't easy to keep your heart pure, to pray for those who have done you wrong, to keep a forgiving spirit in your heart and return good for evil. It is hard to pray for God's will to be done, especially when it applies to your own life. It takes consecration to put God's interests before your own and to walk the narrow way. So, the temptation is to say, "It doesn't matter." It is so much easier to drift along, listening to the voice of inclination instead of the commands of duty. It is so much more pleasant if we leave out all the Gethsemanes and the Calvaries.

But Jesus warns. One winter there is coming a heavy snow up in the mountains. It may be next winter. It may not come for many years. But the very fact that in years past it has come, is proof that it can come again. In the spring that snow will begin to melt, and suddenly one day the nice, dry bed of sand will be filled with a raging torrent which will sweep to destruction the house built there. But the house up on the rocks will still be standing when the flood has passed.

Every person is building. The thoughts you think, the dreams of your heart, the words you speak, the things you do, are the materials which are making up the structure of your life. In His story of the two houses Jesus does not say some are good and some are bad. It goes much deeper than that. He says, some are wise and some are foolish. Because, says He, some day there is coming a testing time.

We can go along fooling ourselves and fooling

other people. But when the flood comes, what one really is, is revealed. Wrong in a life won't stand. And beyond the tests of life itself, is the judgment of the Almighty God.

THE TESTING TIME

It is thrilling to hear Jesus describe the testing of the house which was built upon the rock. He says, "And the rain descended, and the floods came, and the winds blew, and beat upon that house; and it fell not." There you have a picture of strength and stability, of character and courage. Nothing is grander than to see a life stand up when the crises come. Some go to pieces, some break down, some try to run away, but some have built their lives out of the stuff which can stand up and take it.

My greatest earthly inspiration was the life my father built. Into his character he put many materials. There was good humor. He never forgot how to laugh. There was kindness. The people of his churches liked to talk to him when they were in trouble. I never knew him to tell a lie, or in any way be dishonest. Into his life he built love, and he never held the wrong spirit toward another person. He was a very humble man who never learned how to promote himself. I don't think he wanted to learn that.

It happened that I was with him when the floods descended. His local physician had referred him to a cancer specialist in Atlanta. I went with him for the examination and spent many hours with him in the hospital room. He knew the doctor was not doing anything for him except an occasional bit of medicine for the pain. He understood that it would be only a short time.

But never did he show any fear or bitterness. Never did he question the goodness or mercy of God. Because of the way he lived, he was not afraid to die. He had no last minute preparations to make. When the floods came, he was on the rock. The only thing he told me to see about was, if we put anything on his tombstone, he wanted the words: "He was a good man."

Since then the first Psalm has come alive for me. That Psalm describes the good man. It is a man who builds his life on the laws of God. The Psalmist says, "his leaf also shall not wither." The godly man is like the evergreen. In the springtime of the year when all the trees are putting on their new dresses, the evergreen is not very impressive. It has the same old clothes. And during the summertime when all the trees are at their fullest, the evergreen is very inconspicuous.

Neither are we impressed with the evergreen in the autumn when the frost has come and turned the leaves of the other trees into a riot of color. In comparison to the crimson and gold of its neighbors, the evergreen seems mighty drab and colorless. But wait. Here come the cold winds of winter. The sleet lies heavy on the trees. The gayly-colored leaves turn to brown and fall, leaving their trees bare and ugly. But the evergreen is still just the same.

Of course, I think that the life consecrated to Christ is the most beautiful all the time. There are some who disagree. But there comes a time when, more than anything else, we want to sing "Rock of Ages, cleft for me, Let me hide myself in Thee."

17. OUR HERE DETERMINES OUR HEREAFTER

The Parable of the Rich Man and Lazarus

LUKE 16:19-31

JESUS TOLD US ABOUT TWO MEN IN ORDER TO ILLUSTRATE the fact that how we live here determines how we live in the hereafter. All He tells us about the man who went to heaven was that he was poor and sick. So we cannot learn much from him. If that is all it takes, then we do not need churches and preachers to teach us how to get to heaven.

Most of us have done a pretty good job at remaining poor and before we die, we are almost certain to be sick. So to learn the lessons of Jesus' story, we must study the man who went to hell. It is upon him that our Lord puts the spotlight. To begin with, we are told that he was rich. But just being rich was not the reason he went to hell. Later on in this same story we see that Abraham was in heaven and he was one of the richest men of the Bible.

As far as we know Dives earned his wealth honestly. Certainly he was not a miser, because we are told he lived "sumptuously." No doubt he invited his friends

to share with him the things his money could buy. He
likely was known as a good fellow and was very popular.
But notice that Jesus says he "fared sumptuously every
day." Underscore the words "every day," and you will
know a lot about this man.

One day out of seven was the Lord's day. Then,
throughout the year there were certain other days that
were set apart as sacred and holy. Those who loved God
observed His days as special times to pray and to worship. But here was a man who reached the point where
he did not need God. A holy day was no different for
him. There you have revealed the man's character. Not
caring for God, neither did he care for his opportunities
of service to others and his responsibilities. He felt
quite sufficient unto himself and for himself he lived.

One day he died. How his will read we are not told.
Maybe he left his money for good causes. It could be
that his relatives spent the remainder of their days fight-
ing over it. One thing is certain, he left it. One second
after he drew his last breath, he was a rich man no longer.
He had depended on his money for his security and his
happiness. Now, in death, he had nothing.

How well it would have been for him had he listened when Jesus warned: "Lay up for yourselves
treasures in heaven, where neither moth or rust doth
corrupt, and where thieves do not break through nor
steal" (Matt. 6:20).

Whatever else death might mean, it means that we
are stripped from this body of ours. Here we judge
people by their reputations, their possessions, their social distinctions. Many depend on their physical attrac-
tiveness, their brains and abilities. They may get along

fine—until death. And then what? All of those things are gone. We become naked souls. We can neglect God and His claims upon our lives. If we do, Jesus says we will go to hell.

DEATH, THE SEPARATOR

A man once said, "I would give a fortune to know what happens to a man five minutes after he dies." By reading the story of Dives and Lazarus there is a lot we can learn about what happens when one dies. To begin with, we learn that the dead still live and are still themselves. There are those who think that at death we go into a long sleep in which we remain until some trumpet is sounded. Then we all rise for the judgment.

But as you read Jesus' story you see that Dives was very alive immediately after death. He was concerned about the well-being of his five brothers who had not died. He wanted something done for them. We remember how Moses and Elijah came back from the other side to meet with Jesus and three of His disciples on the mountain. (Mark 9). Surely they were alive. Jesus said to the penitent thief as they were both dying, "Today shalt thou be with me in paradise" (Luke 23:43). I think that immediately after death we enter the next life.

After death Dives felt pain, he remembered, he pled for mercy. When he speaks of himself, he says, "I." Though he had been stripped of his physical body and possessions, though he was gone from this earth, he was still "I." All of us will be consciously alive after death. Death makes a lot of changes in the life of a person, but it does not change the person.

If you are saved here, you will be saved there. If

you are without God here, you will be without God there. The only difference death makes is it separates people and some go to hell and some go to heaven. Not only in the story of Dives and Lazarus, but in many places does Jesus make that plain. He said, "And these shall go away into everlasting punishment: but the righteous into life eternal" (Matt. 25-46).

He tells about how the wheat and the tares grow together, but in the harvest they are separated, the tares are burned and the wheat is gathered into the barn (Matt. 13:30). He tells about people going where "there shall be weeping and the gnashing of teeth" (Matt. 22:13). We sometimes say piously, "After all, we are working for the same place." The tragic truth about us is we are not. Death is the great separator of mankind. Jesus says that between heaven and hell "there is a great gulf fixed: so that they which would pass from hence to you cannot; neither can they pass to us, that would come from thence."

In hell Dives pled but he received this reply: "Son, remember that thou in thy lifetime receivedst thy good things, and likewise Lazarus evil things: but now he is comforted, and thou art tormented." What does that mean? Simply that in this life Dives deliberately turned his back on God and the claims of God on his life. He lived for himself, but in death he could not save himself. On the other hand, we remember that in Bible times people were given names which described their characters. The name Lazarus meant "God is my help."

Many believe there is another chance after death. I hope there is. But Jesus does not say so. The tenderest lips the world has ever known spoke of the shut door and the outer darkness and the unquenchable fire. But none of us intend to go to hell. Instead, we like to believe that God is so good and loving He will pat us all on the head and say, "I didn't expect you to be perfect, run along in my House and enjoy yourself." But there are two things which must be said about that.

THE PREPARATION OF OUR SOULS

(1) This life is a preparation for the next, and without the capacity to enjoy it, even heaven would be hell. Two men went to a concert of very fine music. One had studied music for years and as the works of the masters were played, he found great delight in it. The other man knew nothing about music and had developed no capacity for its enjoyment. He sat there bored and uninspired.

I have a friend who went deep into the heart of Africa to be a missionary. Before he left I helped to get up some things for him to carry. One thing he especially wanted was a refrigerator, and he got one that would operate on kerosene. He bought many things to carry along that would enable him to enjoy some of the comforts of life to which he had become accustomed.

His preparation however, went far deeper than the few things he accumulated. He went to school to study the language of the people, to know their customs and their ways of thinking. When he got there, he wanted to be at home with his new friends. He wanted to be able to live with them happily.

As primitive people thought of their journey into

the next life, they felt they must carry with them the things of this life. The Indians, for example, would bury their dead with various articles such as bows and arrows, cooking utensils, and the like. But we realize the fact that we cannot carry with us anything from "hence to yonder." Instead, our preparation must be the preparing of our souls, the cultivating of our tastes for God. Without that preparation, heaven for us becomes an impossibility.

Someone has pictured life as a series of rooms leading one into the other. We go from home to school, from school to college, from college into business, and into marriage and so on all the way through. Until finally we come to the end of this life. What then? Across the centuries comes floating to us the sweetest voice the world has ever known, saying, "I am the door."

And we remember: "For God so loved the world that He gave His only begotten Son, that whosoever believeth in Him should not perish, but have everlasting life" (John 3:16).

18. WHAT JESUS SAID ABOUT
THE JUDGMENT DAY

The Parable of the Last Judgment
MATTHEW 25:31-46

WHAT DID JESUS SAY ABOUT THE JUDGMENT DAY? FOR AN
answer let us study His words as recorded in Matthew
25:31-46. In the first place He said there is going to be
such a day. He says, "When the Son of man shall come
in his glory, and all the holy angels with him, then shall
he sit upon the throne of his glory: And before him
shall be gathered all nations."

Why is it we have so much crime? Is it because the
criminal does not know he is breaking the law? No, it
is because he does not believe he will get caught. When
a man murders or steals, he knows it is against the law.
But he also knows there are many unsolved murders
and uncaught thieves. So he decides he, too, can get by
with it. If every person were sure, perfectly sure, that
every time he breaks the law he would be caught and
tried for it in a court that would be fair but also stern,
most if not all of our law-breaking would cease.

I drive my car about the city a great deal. I've seen
people run a red light, exceed the speed limit, pass on

the wrong side. But when a police car is in sight, I have never seen a person do any of these things. When the policeman stops at the red light, all the others stop. None go around him and cross on a red light. When the policeman drives along the street at the maximum speed limit, no cars pass him. It is when we think the police are not looking, that we take chances with the law.

So with the laws of God. We know what is right and what is wrong. But we refuse to face the fact that someday there is going to be a judgment. Sometimes in our courts of law, even though one has been caught in some crime, by cleverness he can "beat the rap." But no person in his right mind can decide that he can outwit God, the judge of all the universe. "Be not deceived; God is not mocked: for whatsoever a man soweth, that shall he also reap." (Galatians 6:7).

The very process of living makes every day a judgment day. A little boy and a little girl go into a store to buy something for themselves. The boy will likely buy a gun, and the girl will buy a doll. In the act of choosing, they reveal what they are. Two people go into the library to get a book. One selects a book that is of value, that has meaning and purpose and is uplifting. The other selects a book that is sordid and cheap and is degrading. They are not judging the books, the books are judging them.

There is a story about a man who visited an art gallery. As he looked at the work of the great masters he said to the attendant, "I don't think the pictures are so good." The attendant replied, "Excuse me sir, the pictures are not on trial." Likewise, a man might go to a concert of great music and afterward say he was bored. He forgets that he is not the judge of the music, the music is the judge of him. As day by day we have opportunity to decide for God or against Him, our very decisions are God's judgments upon us.

So, when we come to that place that divides this life from the next, there God will be standing and upon us He will put His judgments. Of that we can be sure.

WE WILL BE SURPRISED

When Jesus tells us about the Judgment Day, He says we are going to be surprised. To some He will say, "I was a hungered, and ye gave me meat: I was thirsty and ye gave me drink. . . ." But some will ask the Lord when they did all that for Him. They have no recollection of it. On the other hand, there will be those who failed God and they, too, will not remember when. But God doesn't forget. The Psalmist says, "The judgments of the Lord are true" (19:9).

Someone likens the Judgment Day to the paying of a hotel bill. I spend a good bit of time in hotels, and I know what that means. After five days when you go to pay your bill, you figure it will be $30.00 because the room is $6.00 a day. However, when the clerk hands you your bill it is $43.62. You protest there is some mistake. So he brings out the bookkeeping sheet and begins to read the items off.

You forgot about those two long distance telephone calls you made, and the night when you met an old classmate in the lobby and insisted that he have dinner with you. You signed the check, and it was charged to your room. There was the suit you sent to be cleaned and that morning when you weren't feeling so well and had breakfast sent up. There was an extra charge for that. So when you see the items, you can't argue with the bill.

So the Lord says, "Inasmuch as ye have done it unto one of the least of these my brethren, ye have done it unto me . . . Inasmuch as ye did it not to one of the least of these, ye did it not to me." We may go along leaving God out of our lives, but God does not leave Himself out. If I love somebody, I am also loving God. If I hate somebody, I am hating God. Everything I do, God is involved.

We are not wise enough to choose our own ways so how can we know what God wants us to do? Proverbs tells us, "The fear of the Lord is the beginning of wisdom" (9:10). Fear in that sense does not mean terror such as you would have if you were standing before some tyrant. The fear which is the beginning of wisdom is that which is born of awe, respect and reverence. When you see the majesty of the mountains and the greatness of the sea, you stand in awe of its creator. When you observe the perfection of His laws and the righteousness of His character, your awe rises to respect. When you begin to understand something of His love, your respect rises to deep reverence.

And when one begins to reverence God it begins to show up in the way he lives. Dr. Sockman has said, "The man who does not reverently look up to something or someone higher than himself will let down to things lower than himself." But where is there one person who has lived a life good enough to stand before God on the

Judgment Day? We have all sinned and come short of His glory. What then?

"For God so loved the world, that he gave his only begotten Son, that whosoever believeth on him should not perish, but have everlasting life" (John 3:16). When we come to the final Judgment Day, our only hope is to come singing, "Just as I am, without one plea, But that Thy blood was shed for me."

WE WILL BE SEPARATED

When Jesus tells us about the Judgment Day, He says, "And he shall separate them one from another . . . and he shall set the sheep on his right hand, but the goats on the left." The Judgment Day is a day of separation. Sometimes we wonder why God allows certain people to live and prosper. During the last war some people asked, "Why doesn't God kill Hitler?"

We remember Jesus telling about the servants who asked if they should go and pull out the tares in the fields. The owner of the fields said, "Nay; lest while ye gather up the tares, ye root up also the wheat with them." Then he adds, "Let both grow together until the harvest" (Matt. 13:24-30). Jesus said the Kingdom of Heaven is like that. The rain falls on the just and the unjust but one day comes the separation. Martin Luther had a way of asking, "What will God say about it in the end?" That is the time that really matters.

And what a complete separation it is. Jesus says, "Then shall the King say unto them on his right hand, Come, ye blessed of my Father, inherit the kingdom prepared for you from the foundation of the world."

That is a wonderful promise. Usually we think of the Judgment with trembling and fear, but for many people it is the bright and shining star in the midst of the darkness.

SOME WILL BE GLAD

It thrilled my heart last Thanksgiving morning to see the church filled to overflowing with people who had come to sing praises unto God. But among the many I saw a couple who had only one child. He was a fine boy and in him all their dreams and hopes were vested. He finished college, was called into the service of his country and sent to Korea. Not long ago a telegram came from Washington beginning, "We regret to inform you. . . ." Their boy was gone.

Also in the congregation I saw a lovely lady of some fifty years. I knew she would be eating Thanksgiving dinner alone. The deepest desire of her heart has been for love and a home and children. But during the years when she might have married and started that home, it fell her lot to support and care for an invalid mother.

Also, I saw at the Thanksgiving service a man dressed in very cheap clothes. He has had a hard time and more than once has been sentenced to jail. I do not excuse what he has done, but I happen to know that he grew up in a home without a mother. He missed the love to which every child has a right. Nobody was ever kind to him. The only opportunity he had was what a little dirty boy growing up on the streets might get for himself.

As we sang the Thanksgiving hymns, I found myself saying, "Thank God for the judgment." I am so thankful that someday, some blessed day, our Heavenly Father will see that justice is done. God has all eternity to make things right.

But there is another side to the judgment. Listen to the words of Christ: "Then shall he say also unto them on the left hand, Depart from me, ye cursed, into ever-lasting fire, prepared for the devil and his angels." We do not like to think about it, but the One who loved us enough to die for us, spoke of the shut door, the outer darkness and the unquenchable fire.

19. HIS KINGDOM IS GROWING

The Parable of a Grain of Mustard Seed
LUKE 13:18-19; MATTHEW 13:31-32; MARK 4:30-32

IN JUST A SINGLE SENTENCE, JESUS GAVE US THE METHOD of the establishment of God's kingdom on earth. "It is like a grain of mustard seed, which a man took, and cast into his garden; and it grew, and waxed a great tree; and the fowls of the air lodged in the branches of it."

Near where I live is a concrete sidewalk which is broken and ruined. In grading for that walk probably heavy and impressive machinery was used. The earth was leveled, the rocks were broken and heavy concrete was poured. Unnoticed was a tiny sprout, maybe it was just a seed. Surely it would amount to nothing crushed and buried under concrete. But that seed or sprout began to grow and from the ground it lifted a section of that sidewalk until it broke open and set that growing plant free.

What a tiny little seed God planted at Bethlehem. Just a baby born of an obscure woman from Nazareth. Even as He grew He attracted very little attention for thirty years. As a young man He went around preaching about love and righteousness, about a Father and a new birth. In that day there were so many things so much more important to think about. They had to worry about the oppression of a dictator and high taxes, about building an army and the price of food, about business conditions, houses to live in, clothes to wear.

Finally He attracted enough attention to become a nuisance to a few leaders. They would put a stop to His silly talk. How? They would simply let the big and impressive machinery of the mighty Roman empire bury Him. That was done. He was forgotten. Leslie Weatherhead quotes a vivid passage from "The Procurator of Judea." Lamia is speaking:

"I knew a Jewess . . . Some months after I lost sight of her, I learned by chance that she had attached herself to a small company of men and women who were followers of a young Galilean thaumaturgist. His name was Jesus; he came from Nazareth, and he was crucified for some crime, I don't quite know what. Pontius, do you remember anything about the man?" Pontius Pilate contracted his brows, and his hand rose to his forehead in the attitude of one who probes the deeps of memory. Then after a silence of some seconds: "Jesus?" he murmured. "Jesus—of Nazareth? I cannot call him to mind."

There were a few people however, in whose mind that Jesus was planted. They kept talking about Him and for it they were persecuted, many were killed, but the ones left kept talking. Like the mustard seed, their movement grew. A tiny church was organized, then an-

IN THE LIFE OF A MAN

I was pressed for time the other day as I drove down to Augusta for a speaking engagement. Yet I could not pass through Thomson without seeing Brother J. O. Brand. He is nearly eighty years old now. His hair is snow white. He was sitting on the porch, and when I got out of my car he called out, "Come on in Charles, I'm glad to see you." Hearing his voice made me feel good. Together we talked for a little while and I went on.

For four years I was the pastor of a church in Thomson, and during those four years Brother Brand was my pastor. After long years in the active ministry he had come there to live. He knew more about theology than I did. He was on much more intimate terms with God than I. He was kind and helpful to his young pastor. St. Paul told us the fruit of the Spirit is love, joy, peace, long-suffering, gentleness, goodness, faith, meekness and temperance (Galatians 5:22-23). As I watched the life of Brother Brand I could see all those fruits ripened. His legs are a bit wobbly now. To walk he uses a contraption which he pushes along in front. His body cannot serve him now like it used to. But as we sat together I thought of Jesus' story of how the kingdom of God is like the mustard seed.

Many times has Brother Brand told me how God first came into his life. He was a simple country boy about fourteen years of age. One morning as the preacher explained the word of God at the old camp meeting in Cherokee County, that boy felt a pull on his heart. As the last hymn was sung, he slipped outside the arbor and knelt by a tree. There he made his peace with God. Perhaps no one took notice of him, but the seed was planted in his heart.

It began to grow, and he was inspired to keep on in school until he finished at Old Emory. Through the years he continued his search for the truth. Many hours I have spent with him and from him I have always learned. Not only did he increase in knowledge, but also in spirit. Now at eighty he is serene and unafraid. He doesn't have any money. When he dies no one will be excited over his will. But there are millionaires who would give their last dollars for the peace that is his.

As I drove away I found myself saying, "Lord, make the whole world like Brother Brand." Then we would not be worrying about war; the law of love would be in charge. It would be unnecessary for races to argue in court about their rights, the law of kindness would be sufficient. Men and women would not be haunted by fear, the presence of God would give power. Instead of a conscience burdened by guilt, there would be the peace of a clean heart. Instead of looking back upon a life of regret, there would be the welcome words, "enter thou into the joy of thy lord."

It is marvelous to think how a tiny acorn can grow into a mighty oak tree. It is far more marvelous to realize how God coming into the heart of a simple country boy can produce a Brother Brand. And not him alone. It can do as much for me—for you—for the whole world.

20. FOR THOSE WHO ARE WAITING FOR A CHANCE

The Parable of the Laborers

MATTHEW 20:1-16

DURING A QUESTION AND ANSWER PERIOD THE OTHER night, someone asked me the meaning of the verse: "So the last shall be first, and the first last: for many be called, but few chosen." Jesus made that statement at the conclusion of a very interesting, yet somewhat confusing, parable. A man went out early in the morning to hire laborers for his vineyard who were to begin work immediately, about six o'clock. Three hours later he saw some other men standing idle in the market place and hired them. Six hours later he hired others and nine hours later still others. Even at the eleventh hour he hired some men to work.

At the close of the day the laborers came for their pay. The owner of the vineyard had agreed to pay the ones who started early in the morning a penny a day for their services. They were satisfied with that wage, and if they had been paid first and dismissed, we would have heard nothing else from them.

Instead, the owner first called those who had

worked only one hour and paid them a penny. Each of the other laborers was also paid a penny. The ones who had worked all day grumbled and said it was not fair. To pay those who worked only one hour the same amount as those who had borne the burden of the heat of the day does seem a little unjust. But Jesus told the story to illustrate some great truths in regard to man's service to God. Let's see what lessons He meant us to learn from it.

First, the word "idle" referring to the men in this story does not mean lazy nor loafing. Rather does it mean "workless." The reason they were not working is not because they did not want to work. Rather was it because they could not find an opportunity. The fact they were standing in the market place indicates they were seeking employment. If they had not wanted work, they would have stayed at home.

To their credit may it be said they never gave up. Imagine waiting eleven hours hoping for an opportunity. The waiting took more courage than the working. And finally when an opportunity did come, though it was the eleventh hour, they did not say, "Well, it's too late to start now." Instead they went and did their best in the time left. Here is the important lesson, they were given credit not only for the work they did, but also for the work they would have done had they had the opportunity. Jesus says God so deals with us.

There was David. He lived a full life, but the thing he wanted most to do was to build the great temple. In this he failed. However, God said, "Whereas it was in thine heart to build a house unto my name, thou didst well that it was in thine heart" (I Kings 8:18). God counts not only our accomplishment, but also our dreams. David did all he could toward building the temple and died disappointed. There are many people who would do much more with their lives, but they are kept waiting in the market place. God understands the pain of disappointment.

THERE IS A PAY DAY

In Jesus' story of the laborers in the vineyard, those who came at the eleventh hour were paid the same as those who worked all day. That brings up the question of God's reward for the faithful. There is an old sixteenth-century prayer which says: "Teach us to labor and not to ask for any reward save that of knowing that we do thy will." But if you read the New Testament, you will find Jesus talking quite a bit about rewards— "Great is your reward in heaven" (Matt. 5.12), "He shall in no wise lose his reward" (Matt. 10:42), "Your reward shall be great" (Luke 6:35), "Thy Father . . . shall reward thee openly" (Matt. 6:4). God promises reward for those who serve Him.

Weatherhead quotes an old Spanish proverb which says: "Take what you want, take it and pay for it." Life is about like that. We have freedom to "take what we want." If one chooses sin, eventually there is a pay day. If one follows God, there is also a pay day. If the pay is bad, we call it consequences, if the pay is good, we call it reward. As to the reward one receives, God decides. Many we put last, God will put first because He knows all the circumstances. "Man looketh on the outward appearance, but the Lord looketh on the heart" (I Sam. 16:7).

Here are two young women both of whom wish to dedicate their lives as missionaries. One goes to school, is sent to the mission field and renders a conspicuous service. The mother of the other suddenly becomes ill and is an invalid for many years. Her daughter must stay and care for her. After many years the mother dies but now the daughter must content herself with less thrilling service. The world may judge the service of the two differently, but God knows better how to judge.

Suppose, however, because the second girl could not enter the field of service she had planned, she had become bitter and resentful. And that is a very real temptation. There are a lot of people who say, "I missed the bus, there is nothing left for me." It isn't hard to serve. The very service itself is a thrilling experience. What is far harder is waiting for the chance.

We like football. It is a rough game in which the player takes some hard knocks, but there is a thrill about it. There is the cheering of the crowd, the write-ups in the paper, the satisfaction of playing the game. The hardest position to play on the football team is sitting on the bench. Nobody applauds the bench sitter. All he can do is wait, hoping for a chance to play.

The good substitute remains ready whenever the coach calls. And in the great game of life, it seems that God keeps a lot of people waiting. But be assured He doesn't forget us, and He would have us remain free of bitterness. It is ours to do our best under the circumstances and leave the rewards to Him.

GOD KNOWS WHO IS WAITING

Jesus concludes the parable of the workers in the vineyard in which those who came in at the eleventh hour were paid the same as those who worked all day with the statement, "For many are called, but few are chosen." This phrase was clearly understood by those who heard Him because it referred to the ancient Roman custom of recruiting their armies. In that day they did not draft people into the army as we do. Instead, service in the army was the highest honor which could come to one. The dream of every little boy was that he be chosen for service.

Rome did not accept volunteers for the army, instead they were chosen. We select our boys to enter our academies at Annapolis and West Point much the same way. When there is a vacancy, a number of boys may be called to take the examination. But out of those selected, only one may be chosen. The others must go back maybe to try again next year, or maybe never to get another chance.

The various political sub-divisions of Rome selected their candidates each year, but out of the group presented, only a few were chosen. The others returned to their homes to serve in other ways. In the eyes of their neighbors, and in their own eyes, they were failures. But not so in the kingdom of God. God rewards all men according to their spirit and the state of their heart. We judge each other by results. God judges by intentions.

In the early morning the workers would go to the market place and stand and wait for the land-owners to come to hire their laborers for the day. There were usually more workers than there were jobs, so some would be left out. Probably some would deeply resent not being selected. Likely one would be heard saying, "I am more worthy than that one who was chosen." Maybe in resentment he would go home. But others stayed on hoping for a chance. Some stayed on and were not chosen until the eleventh hour. But at the end of the day their reward was just as great. As someone has said, "They also serve who stand and wait."

It is hard to stay in lesser places and keep a sweet and humble spirit when you see others getting ahead. Many feel their chance has forever gone. But be assured that God knows we are waiting, and may we keep our lives fresh and ready for Him. Not spoiled by resentment or envy. It is true that in life "few are chosen," but in God's kingdom, all are chosen. To hear Him say, "Well done, thou good and faithful servant . . . enter thou into the joy of thy Lord" (Matt. 25:21).

When asked the secret of his success in the Salvation Army, General William Booth said: "I will tell you the secret. God has had all there was of me. There have been men with greater brains than I, men with greater opportunities. But I made up my mind God should have all of William Booth there was."

21. OVERCOME THE EVIL OF LIFE

*The Parable of the Wheat
and the Tares*

MATTHEW 13:24-30

WALK WITH ME DOWN THE HALL OF A GREAT HOSPITAL. In this room there is a mother and a newborn baby. Standing with them is the father. There is a fine couple who have lived good lives. They rejoiced over their coming baby. Now it is here but was born blind. The parents are heartbroken. Why did God let that happen?

In another room is a young man almost bent double with pain. He has cancer in such a stage nothing can be done for him. We visit a young lady in her teens stricken with polio. She will be crippled the rest of her life. Here is a dear woman suffering from arthritis. Why does God allow disease in this world He has created?

Sit with me in my study. In walks a young woman, the mother of two children. She was so happy until one night the phone rang to tell the news that her husband had been killed in an accident. Why did God let that happen? Another comes with the blight of a great disappointment, another in a situation which is destroying all chance of happiness. Why doesn't God prevent such things?

We read in the paper of a hurricane that kills people, destroys homes and property. Earthquakes shake a city to pieces. A drought hangs on so long that farmers lose everything and people go hungry. Surely God knows about these injustices of nature. Why does He let them continue?

More especially, there is the fact of sin, of evil desires, of temptations on every hand. Lives are blighted, the conscience is burdened, both the innocent and the guilty are made to suffer. Why? Surely God is stronger than evil. If He loves us and is concerned about us, why doesn't He take out of our lives all temptations and set us free? Why does He tolerate evil?

The Bible teaches that God created this universe, that nothing exists apart from His creation. The Bible also teaches that God is good and is kind and is loving. We also are taught that God has infinite knowledge and infinite power. But how can we reconcile blind babies, cancer, polio, accidents, hurricanes, the existence of sin and all the other evils of the world with a loving, all-powerful creator, God?

Sometimes the evil of the world causes people to doubt that God cares about the individual. Sometimes evil causes one to doubt the goodness of God. Sometimes, evil even causes one to doubt the existence of God. Walter de la Mare wrote a poem, "The Listeners," in which he wonders if really there is "Anybody there." The other day I heard a little crippled boy singing, "I am so glad that Jesus loves me," but sometimes we cannot help but wonder.

We are not surprised that even the great Carlyle

would exclaim, "God sits in heaven and does nothing," or that the Psalmist would plead, "Keep not thou silence, O God: hold not thy peace, and be not still, O God. For, lo, thine enemies make a tumult" (83:1,2).

CONCENTRATE ON THE WHEAT

In facing the problem of evil in the world, Jesus gave us a parable. A man had a field in which he had sowed good seed. While he slept an enemy came and sowed tares among the wheat. After the wheat and the tares had grown enough to be recognized, the servants wanted to go immediately and pull out the tares. But the owner said no because in so doing they would also uproot the wheat. Instead, let them grow together until the harvest, and there they will be separated.

When we face the evil of the world, we wonder why God does not root it out. If evil is not God's will, then let Him remove it now, we say. We heard it said again and again, "Why doesn't God strike Hitler dead?" Some people even prayed for that to happen, but they really did not want their prayer answered. Hitler in our minds represented evil, and what we were saying was that God should destroy the evil.

But we must remember that God is impartial and fair in His dealings with men. Hitler was evil, but so are we. Every one of us is a bewildering mixture of good and evil. Even in those first disciples, the twelve Christ chose for his intimate friends, we see the tares growing with the wheat—cowardice, selfishness, harsh judgments and unkind criticisms. How much more true is it of you and me that along with what good we possess there is also much evil.

God rejects the method of the servants. They wanted to focus their attention just on the evil and root it out. But since the good and the evil in the world and in human life are so bound together, the rooting of it out would destroy us. Sickness and health, sorrow and joy, sin and righteousness, hate and love, life and death—they all grow from the same roots. Destroy the possibility of one and you also destroy the possibility of the other.

Instead of pulling out the tares, a purely negative method, Jesus concentrated on the wheat. He would encourage and sustain the best within us and our world until we had fulfilled the remedy of St. Paul, "Be not overcome of evil, but overcome evil with good" (Romans 12:21). Jesus said, "In the world ye shall have tribulation: but be of good cheer; I have overcome the world" (John 16:33). Instead of removing the evil, God does something better. He helps us to overcome it.

We must remember the difference in what God allows and what God intends. He allows sin. He does not intend sin. It has been well stated that "the capacity for sin and the capacity for communion with God are the same capacity." The freedom to choose evil and the freedom to choose God is the same freedom. For God to take all the evil out of the world would leave us spineless, jellyfish creatures. But to give us the power to overcome the evil through the cultivation of the good makes us like unto Him who is our God.

"Be of good cheer," Christ said. Never forget, there

is always room for cheer as long as we have faith in and maintain friendship with Him who has overcome the world.

EVIL IS CREATIVE

James S. Stewart quotes a story of a woman who has met a sudden sorrow. "I wish I'd never been made!" she exclaims bitterly. To which her friend quietly replies, "My dear, you're not made yet. You're only being made—and this is the Maker's process." Every great painting has in it shadow as well as light and so does every great life.

As you look back over your own life, ask yourself what experiences have blessed and taught you the most. What would you name first? Some picnic? Some light, carefree hour? No, you would list some sorrow or disappointment, some difficulty or frustrated hope, some dream that flickered and died or some hurt that has left a permanent mark upon your heart. The most creative force in this world is evil.

Evil built our hospitals, our schools, our churches. The pain of sickness, the blight of ignorance and the burden of sin have been creative forces. Because of the pain of walking, we created a way to ride. Because of the suffering that a bitter cold winter can bring, we created a way to heat our houses. Nearly every good we have has come as the result of some evil.

And that is the way we want it. Lessing, the great philosopher, declared that if God came to him, offering in His right hand the whole truth, and in His left the search for truth and all the toil and pain and mistakes of the search, he would still choose the search. Not the finished article but the joy of a work to do was what he wanted. My little boy comes home from school to struggle with his home work. I could quickly and easily do it for him, but I would destroy his life if I did it.

We have all made mistakes. We get ourselves into situations which seem hopeless—some weakness in our lives seems as though it will ruin us—some wrong we have done weighs heavily on our conscience—some pain or physical handicap destroys the joy in living. We feel defeated and hopeless. Then we are reminded to turn to religious faith. Religion is betting our lives there is a God. Through our faith we begin to conquer the evil —our faith is the making of us.

But what about those sorrows that no amount of faith can eliminate? Jesus said, "In the time of harvest I will say to the reapers, Gather ye together first the tares, and bind them in bundles and burn them: but gather the wheat into my barn" (Matt. 13:30). God has an eternity to finish His creation.

If I had to judge all of the experiences of life just on a basis of this world, I would be completely at a loss to believe in the final triumph of God. We believe there is more to follow than just this life, and upon that fact we base our faith and we refuse to surrender to evil. Death did not defeat God in Christ—death became the means to His final triumph. In a world like this, we will, we must link our lives with God.

22. THE IDEA OF POSITIVE THINKING

*The Parable of the House that was
Swept Clean and Left Empty*

MATTHEW 12:43-45

THERE ARE VAST NUMBERS OF PEOPLE WHO ARE DEFEATED
in their lives. Their conqueror may be some wrong
action, or it may be a mental evil, such as fear or worry.
I am convinced that no person need be defeated by anything. Whatever the obstacle in the way of your success
or happiness, on the authority of the wisest man who
ever lived, I declare you have within reach the power
to live victoriously.

There was a lady who rented a jeep to do some
heavy work. Having been told that a jeep could go
anywhere, she drove down on the beach and got mired
up in some soft sand. She raced the motor but instead
of pulling out, the jeep just mired further in the sand.
She walked to a nearby garage to get the wrecker to
come and pull the jeep out.

The garage man explained she did not need the
wrecker, but he went with her to show her what to do.
He pointed to a gearshift lever that she had not noticed
and explained that the jeep has a pulling gear. He

showed her how to operate it, and the jeep pulled right out of the sand. He then commented, "That lady thought she was stuck, but she had more power than she realized. She just wasn't using it."

When God made us, He gave us a "pulling gear." We frequently encounter difficulties which stop our progress and hold us back. We get mired up in some situation or in some circumstances. But within us is a marvelous power that can keep us going. Some people call that power "positive thinking." Jesus used two other terms:

"Believe" was one of the words He used to refer to man's pulling power. He said, "If thou canst believe, all things are possible to him that believeth" (Mark 9:23). Another word He used was "faith." He said, "If ye have faith as a grain of mustard seed, ye shall say unto this mountain, Remove hence to yonder place; and it shall remove: and nothing shall be impossible unto you" (Matt. 17:20). It is the positive action, represented by belief and faith, that gains the victory.

To illustrate the principle of the power of positive action, Jesus gave us a very simple yet graphic story. It is the story of a man's battle with some evil in his life. He says it is like a man who swept the evil spirit out of his house. The spirit wandered around for some time but later came back and found the house "empty, swept and garnished." So the spirit moved back in and brought with him seven other spirits worse than himself. The man ended up in a worse state than he was in to start with (Matt. 12:43-45).

Go back to the woman in the jeep for a moment.

She might have dug away at the sand, but that would not have got her mired jeep out. Instead, she needed to turn on the power to pull through the sand. Just to reform our lives is not enough. Through the use of faith and belief, through positive thinking and action, the weaknesses and sins of our lives are overcome.

AN EMPTY HOUSE WON'T STAY EMPTY

As I read Jesus' story of the man who swept his house clean, driving out the evil spirit (Matt. 12:43-45), I find in my heart real admiration for him. He faced the evil of his life honestly and said, "I will tolerate it no longer. I will drive it out of my life." That takes real courage. He swept his life clean. That is essential.

You never gain power over the weaknesses and wrongs of your life until you face up to them honestly and admit them. Then you must be willing not only to let them go, but also to make whatever effort is required in ridding your life of those things.

This is not easy because you must deal with your mind and your mind is the biggest liar in the world. It will trick you if it can. First it will try to get you to believe that certain things are not wrong. "Other people do those same things, and they get along all right," our minds will tell us. Or the mind may tell you to wait until next year before deciding really to do anything. Or the mind may convince you that you are weak and you can do nothing.

The man in Jesus' story said, "I've lived with this evil thing as long as I intend to. Now I mean to drive it out," and he did. That was good. It is good when you make such a decision. Then the man made a fatal mistake. He concentrated on the evil to be expelled, but he failed to develop the good to take its place.

One trouble with an empty house is it won't stay empty. You can clean it up, move everything out and lock the door but dust will gather in the corners, rats will gnaw their way in, spiders spin their webs, termites go to work on it. I read a lot of ghost stories, and usually the ghosts live in an empty house.

So it is with the house of life. Left empty, uninvited and undesirable tenants move in. In the first world war, the allied armies defeated the Kaiser but did nothing really constructive, and Hitler, who was worse, came in. The Pharisees in Jesus' day cast out the gross sins, but they developed no positive program and self-righteousness and hardness of their hearts took over. Moral reform is good as far as it goes. In fact, it is the first step to the possessing of the power of God. God cannot come into a life until we are willing to renounce our wrongs. But to stop there will result in failure.

If we fail to replace our wrongs with positive good, eventually the wrong will come back with much stronger force. Jesus said, "Believe." That is, create in your mind a picture of the person you want to be. Keep that picture before you, let it occupy your thinking, and there will be no place for thoughts of the evil which will be wanting to come back into your life. It was William James who said, "Believe and your belief will create the fact." That is positive thinking.

A man told me he knew he could quit drinking, because he had quit no less than a hundred times. The problem is not how to put something out of our lives but rather how to keep it out. So often we are like the man in Jesus' story who drove the unclean spirit out but left his house empty, and later not only that spirit, but seven worse spirits moved back in (Matt. 12:43-45).

I know a lady who had a deep fear of flying in an airplane. Her husband showed her very impressive statistics proving that a plane was much safer than a car. She was told how much quicker and more comfortably she could fly. But all the arguments were to no avail. She just could not get the consent of her mind to fly. Once she was far away from home when the message came that her child had suddenly become critically ill. Frantically she phoned the airport for reservations on the next plane. All the way she thanked God for such a quick method of travel. She felt absolutely no fear of it. What conquered her fear? It was the thought of getting to the bedside of her child and the service she could render. Her fear was overcome by positive thinking and action.

Would you like to overcome some evil spirit in your life? It may be some sinful habit, it may be some mental burden such as fear or worry, it may be a feeling of hopelessness and despair. It may be that you do not feel your life is counting for anything. You have tried moral reformation of yourself, the "turning over a new leaf," and resolutions to do better. Now try positive thinking.

Decide some definite accomplishment to give yourself to. It helps to write it down. Keep writing until you can express it in no more than twenty-five words. Then test it according to the will of God. Be sure it is right and just and good. If God would approve it, and you will know, then begin the process of fixing it clearly in your mind. Read it over several times a day until the very thought of it becomes a part of you.

But don't stop with just that. There is one further step. The thing you want to accomplish is likely something that is difficult. Perhaps you feel your strength is unequal to the task. Gain the companionship of one who is sufficient for every task. Listen to the Psalmist: "Yea, though I walk through the valley of the shadow of death," that is, the difficult and hard paths of life, "I will fear no evil," that is, I will not entertain a failure thought of any kind. And how can that be accomplished? "For thou are with me" (Psalm 23).

As we fill our lives with a sense of the presence of God, we overcome our weaknesses and our defeats. Remember the words of St. Paul: "I can do all things through Christ which strengtheneth me" (Philippians 4:13). That is positive thinking at its best.